Cross-Pollination

The Miracle of Unity in Intercession, Revival, and the Harvest

Lila Terhune

Revival Press

An Imprint of
Destiny Image₍ᵣ₎ Publishers, Inc.
P.O. Box 310
Shippensburg, PA 17257-0310

ISBN 0-7684-1004-5

For Worldwide Distribution
Printed in the U.S.A.

Third Printing: 1999   Fourth Printing: 2000

This book and all other Destiny Image, Revival Press, Mercy Place, Fresh Bread, and Treasure House books are available at Christian bookstores and distributors worldwide.

For a U.S. bookstore nearest you, call **1-800-722-6774**.
For more information on foreign distributors,
call **717-532-3040**.
Or reach us on the Internet: **http://www.reapernet.com**

Dedication

So many people have affected my life over the years, and I would love to acknowledge them all. However, I want to dedicate this book particularly to my family, who have had to live with me all these years:

My mother, who has already gone on to be with the Lord.

My father, who received our Lord at 84 years of age, but who has always been a wonderful dad.

Bob, my oldest son, who has a great call upon his life. May he be faithful to it.

Robin, my oldest daughter, who has been a good friend as well as a daughter. May she prophesy God's word to the nations, and serve the youth of this generation.

Tracy, my youngest son, who has always had such a sensitive heart, and whom Jesus visited when he was a young boy and instructed him on prayer.

Rhonda, my baby, whom we dedicated from the womb to serve the Lord. He has preserved her life more than once, for He has a large platform for her in ministry.

My grandchildren, Heather, Jessica, Robby, Jeremy, John, and Skee, and great-grandson Trey, who are the seed that will serve the Lord in the generations to come if He shall tarry.

Cindy, who is my own Ruth.

Maxine, my sister-in-law, who spent many hours pouring into my life.

And last but not least, my husband Bob, without whose love and encouragement I would not have been able to write this book. He has been my confidant and best friend through all the struggles we have experienced. He has believed in me when I didn't believe in my myself. Thank you, my darling.

Endorsements

Lila Terhune has beautifully depicted in her book, *Cross-Pollination*, the work of the Holy Spirit in this present-day revival. Spanning time, distance, and denomination, her unique understanding can by stated no better than in her words: "God is cross-pollinating His Church with glory!"

Ruth Ward Heflin
Calvary Pentecostal Tabernacle
Ashland, Virginia
Author of *Glory* and *Revival Glory*

Lila Terhune has an incredible gift from God to lead intercession. Her perception and spiritual insight have enabled her to bring much revelation to the Body of Christ. We are sure that those who read this book will be helped into deeper levels of prayer. God has raised up certain individuals to motivate and equip the Body of Christ in these awesome days, and Lila is one such person. Her faithfulness to God's call, her humility, and her pursuit of God's glory make her a fine example to us all.

Ken and Lois Gott, Founders
Revival Now! International Ministries

Contents

Foreword

One evening long before revival broke out at Brownsville, I was in the sanctuary praying and the Holy Spirit reaffirmed to me that He was going to do a mighty work in our church. He also strongly impressed upon me that He would send people to help in areas where we needed it. Sure enough, after revival broke out, I began to see those areas that needed someone with a special calling. The Holy Spirit led Bob and Lila Terhune from the West Coast to Brownsville. She is one of those unpaid laborers who helps this mighty revival going night after night.

Prayer is what sparked the Brownsville Revival. Prayer is what perpetuates it. Without prayer, this move would die out—not abruptly, because there would still be enough prayers prayed to carry it for awhile—but soon it would wilt and die back to nothing.

Lila Terhune is not only an intercessor, but also a warrior, a motivator, and an administrator—and is very loyal to leadership. As you read her book, *Cross-Pollination*, you will weep, laugh, make notes, and receive revelations concerning God's plan for these endtimes. This enlightening book concerning intercession will become a handbook to many as they obey a fresh call from the Holy Spirit to stand in the gap and fill their position of duty.

God truly is raising up many to intercede in these last days before judgment falls. In Ezekiel 9:3-4 it says, "…And He called to the man clothed with linen, which had the writer's inkhorn by his side; and the Lord said unto him, Go through the midst of the city, through the midst of Jerusalem, and set a mark upon the foreheads of the men that sigh and that cry for all the abominations that be done in the midst thereof."

The Brownsville Revival can be summed up in one word: *souls*. Yes, backsliders are coming back to God, but many thousands of first-time converts also come running to the mercy seat nightly. Thanks be to God for Lila Terhune and her skilled army of intercessors that stay in the trenches to sigh and cry for all the abominations that are done in the midst thereof.

Intercessors are our unsung heroes. They are the marked ones.

Pastor John Kilpatrick
Brownsville Assembly of God

Foreword

As you read this book, I think you will agree with me that it is highly anointed, exciting, and very challenging. I found myself repenting, wanting more of God's presence and power, and feeling so honored to be a part of His plan.

Lila's energy is contagious! She's a joy to be around. She's a hard worker, a tenacious person, and a great teacher and lover of the Lord.

She is truly the "Queen Bee" of intercession at Brownsville, birthing many intercessors in the hive, encouraging and leading our little bees into the deeper prophetic purposes of God in the earth.

Brenda Kilpatrick
Brownsville Assembly of God

Introduction

Behold, how good and how pleasant it is for brethren to dwell together in unity! It is like the precious oil upon the head, running down on the beard, the beard of Aaron, running down on the edge of his garments. It is like the dew of Hermon, descending upon the mountains of Zion; for there the Lord commanded the blessing—life forevermore (Psalm 133).

When the revival at Brownsville Assembly of God in Pensacola, Florida, began in June 1995, I knew it could possibly be the beginning of the great end-time harvest. When I was invited to organize and coordinate the Intercessory Prayer Department, one of my first concerns was for the Christian community to understand that the Holy Spirit was not simply moving in one local church or city, but that He was moving in many different places in the earth.

It was equally important for Christians to understand that each person enjoying this outpouring of the Holy Spirit would interact with and endorse one another! **Mature** believers understand that each "stream" in God's river has a different purpose, and all are given exclusively for the glory and purposes of God.

The term "cross-pollination" is a botanical term (having to do with the transfer of pollen from one flower to another), but it beautifully describes the way one part, family, or "stream" of God's diverse Kingdom gives and receives from others in the unity that Jesus prayed for in His great high priestly prayer in the garden of Gethsemane (see Jn. 17:20-21).

History tells us that every major move of God was preceded by a return to unity; and unfortunately, virtually every great revival has been followed by disunity. This happens when those most touched by God "make camp" or stop to build monuments to (and walls around) their own experience while disallowing all others.

God in His wisdom never gives any one group of believers "all" truth, and the reason is obvious—even to us! There is only one way for us to become whole and complete as His Body manifested in the earth: We must exchange and fully share our strengths, giftings, and joy in His visitation. In the words of Paul:

> *There is one body and one Spirit, just as you were called in one hope of your calling; one Lord, one faith, one baptism; one God and Father of all, who is above all, and through all, and in you all* (Ephesians 4:4-6).

Even the leadership gifts listed by Paul in the same chapter—apostles, prophets, evangelists, pastors, and teachers— were all given to train us for the ministry, to edify us, and to help us come "to the unity of the faith…to a perfect man, to the measure of the stature of the fullness of Christ" (Eph. 4:12-13).

This book is not intended to be an instruction manual or a "how to" book on intercession, prayer, and revival. It is meant to be an open door into the greater glory of God's plan for the Church. Intercession, prayer, and revival are indeed part of this plan, but there is so much more!

It is my greatest desire that the pages of this book will open the hearts of God's people to the larger picture of what He has purposed for this day. I pray that you will be encouraged to trust the Lord that your prayers are not "laying out there in the empty air somewhere." No, they remain as memorials before God's throne and He will move upon them in His own time.

It has also been a great privilege to give honor and humble tribute to those "giants of faith" who have contributed prayer and sacrifice to the present-day outpouring. These little known heroes laid down their own ambitions and priorities to take up the burden of Christ for our generation. Through their obedience and selfless prayers, they have prophesied "Life and salvation!" to our generation and infused us with overcoming faith to believe for greater things.

We acknowledge our debt to those who went before, and our obligation to those who lie ahead in the fields ripe for harvest. To Jesus Christ the risen Lord, and to God our Father be all the glory!

Chapter 1

Called to the Mountain

Now all the people witnessed the thunderings, the lightning flashes, the sound of the trumpet, and the mountain smoking; and when the people saw it, they trembled and stood afar off (Exodus 20:18).

My life changed forever the day in 1961 when I was handed a copy of a prophecy by a man named Tommy Hicks. That year he had received the same heavenly vision three times in one night. It was a vision in which God revealed that He was going to move mightily around the world in the last days. I read that prophecy while I was still in the United Brethren in Christ Church, about a year before I was baptized in the Holy Spirit. (Although I didn't believe in "prophecy" at the time, somehow I knew that Tommy Hicks had heard from God.)

The 1960's were not happy years for much of the world. In October 1962, the year after I read Tommy Hicks' prophecy, Americans were told that the Soviets had installed nuclear missiles in Cuba, just 90 miles off the coast of the United States. Soviet commanders in Cuba were authorized to use tactical nuclear weapons if invaded, and American troops were poised to do just that. The world literally came to the very brink of nuclear war during that 14-day crisis as President John F. Kennedy challenged Premier Nikita Khrushchev and forced Soviet tankers laden with missiles to turn away from Cuba. That was also the year that I was baptized in the Holy Spirit in the United Brethren in Christ Church of Lakewood, California.

A lot of end-time "prophets" were prophesying that the "end" was near. They assured us that things were going to become darker and more gloomy until everything ended in nuclear holocaust and Armageddon. These "prophets" just knew that they had finally identified the antichrist in Nikita Khrushchev. Everyone thought that the Church would grow so weak that unless believers were removed off of this planet, the Church would be unable to stand or survive. But once I read Tommy Hicks' prophecy, I saw something glorious every time I went to God's Word.

I met Bob that same year, and we were married in 1966. We no longer saw doom and gloom as we looked about us; rather, we saw the promise of God moving in the Church and bringing great revival in the last days. Although this wasn't always popular to preach and teach, we preached it, believed it, and prayed for it anyway. By the Spirit, we were seeing God's glory being *returned* to the Church. We sensed that somehow God would move mightily and we would see the Holy Spirit sweep thousands and thousands into the Kingdom by His power. Over and over again, certain passages from Tommy Hicks' prophecy would come to mind and ignite my passion for God's glory to cover the earth:

"At that very moment there came a great thunder that seemed to roar from the heavens. I turned my eyes toward the heavens and suddenly I saw a figure in white, in glistening white—the most glorious thing that I have ever seen in my entire life. I did not see the face, but somehow I knew it was the Lord Jesus Christ, and He stretched forth His hand, and as He did, He would stretch it forth to one, and to another, and to another. And as He stretched forth His hand upon the nations and the people of the world—men and women—as He pointed toward them, this liquid light seemed to flow from His hands into them, and a mighty anointing of God came upon them, and those people began to go forth in the name of the Lord...

"God is going to give the world a demonstration in this last hour as the world has never known. These men and women are of all walks of life, degrees will mean nothing. I saw these workers as they were going over the face of the earth. When one would stumble and fall, another would come and pick him up. There was no 'big I' and 'little you,' but every mountain was brought low and every valley was exalted, and they seemed to have one thing in common—there was a divine love, a divine love that seemed to flow forth from these people as they worked together, and as they lived together. It was the most glorious sight that I have ever known. Jesus Christ was the theme of their life. They continued and it seemed the days went by as I stood and beheld this sight. I could only cry, and sometimes I laughed. It was so wonderful as these people went throughout the face of the whole earth, bringing forth in this last end time.

"As I watched from the very heaven itself, there were times when great deluges of this liquid light seemed to fall upon great congregations, and that congregation would lift up their hands and seemingly praise God for hours and even days as the Spirit of God came upon them. God said, 'I will pour My Spirit upon all flesh,' and that is exactly this thing. And to every man and every woman that received this power, and the anointing of God, the miracles of God, there was no ending to it."[1]

The Secret of the Open Heavens

I knew that Tommy Hicks had conducted tremendously successful revivals in Argentina in the 1950's, and one morning I shared this information in my Sunday school class. Afterward, a visiting pastor from Adelaide, Australia, named Phil Lowe, came up to talk with me. He said, "Lila, the story goes back farther than that. It goes back to a missionary by the name of Ed Miller, who went to Argentina in the late 40's." That reminded me of something else I'd heard about Argentina, and I said, "Is this the missionary who had the prayer meeting that caused the open heaven to come into the area?" He said, "The very one."

I felt a surge of anointing when I heard Pastor Lowe's answer because I'd heard about Ed Miller. "Is this man still alive?" I asked, and he said, "I believe he is." Later on he sent me Dr. Ed Miller's address. (This gentleman is in his 80's and living in Georgia at this writing.)

With a little effort, I was able to meet Dr. Miller and get the Argentina story straight from him. I learned that he had written some wonderful books that describe his prolific ministry in which he witnessed seven great revivals and saw God turn entire nations from darkness to light. It turned out that God used Dr. Miller's persistent intercessory ministry with Argentine believers to break satan's hold on their country and to pave the way for Tommy Hicks' crusade three years later! The parallels to our situation today are extremely important, as God's Spirit is currently hovering over the nations of the world.

Dr. Miller told me that Argentina was tightly closed to the gospel when he arrived in the 1940's. In the foreword to his book, *Cry for Me Argentina*, Dr. Miller describes the obstacles that he faced as a missionary in a country with "heavens of brass," and these passages are chillingly similar to descriptions of the United States and many other nations around the world today:

> "When I first went to Argentina it was a country prosperous in material things. However, its religion had become so degraded that the priesthood was corrupt to the core. The Argentine people had lost faith in their religion and few attended their temples.... The few evangelical missionaries had made no impact at all on the nation. They were mostly unknown, and when known, they were derided and mocked. Argentina had no God. The Argentine people were totally indifferent to anything that had to do with religion. Their indifference created a religious vacuum which was ripe for any religion, even communism, to enter.

"My own first experience as a missionary was no better than any other missionary's...Argentina was known in missionary circles as the hardest field in the western hemisphere...in Argentina—I was a failure. I was seriously thinking of leaving and perhaps finding a more fruitful form of employment when I heard within my spirit, 'CRY FOR ME, ARGENTINA!' Hearing these words, I realized there was no one crying for God to come to that land. I knew that if Argentina would cry for God, He would come to her.

"Argentina heard...and cried, and cried and cried for her God to come to her. And the Merciful God and Savior of men heard her cry."[2]

Ed Miller did what most missionaries do when they establish a work on a mission field—he evangelized. He and another missionary visited villages and towns and set up tents for meetings. Then they would pass out tracts and visit with every living soul in these places for weeks on end—and never see a single person visit their meetings. They fasted and prayed, they strategized and agonized, but nothing happened. Then the Lord began to deal with Dr. Miller about intimacy with Him.

The Way of Power

The heavens were closed, and the missionary had tried everything that he had been trained to do. At first he blamed everyone and everything else but himself, but then, as he writes, "The long road of excuses was over. My fleeing ended. God caused me to take inventory of myself—the result was disillusioning. Bitterly defeated, all defenses overthrown, I was brought by God into a conference of surrender."[3] Dr. Miller said he realized that "flesh works" were unacceptable, even if they had the stamp of acceptable religion. He said, "God was offering a new way—a way of power—an operation of the Holy Spirit Himself released in the ministry of deliverance."[4]

He felt that the Lord wanted him to spend at least eight hours a day in prayer and the Word, just as if it was his "job." Despite criticism and open disapproval from people who thought that he ought to be doing traditional missionary activities to earn his salary, Miller prayed. He refused to go one step further until he had answered God's challenge to prayer.

At one point, God dropped a nugget of wisdom into Miller's spirit about fasting, "Fasting is not the coin of Heaven," and Miller thought, *I wish the Lord had told me that the first day.* From then on, he concentrated on seeking God's face instead of His hand, but it wasn't easy. Anyone who has fasted or prayed for extended periods will relate to Dr. Miller's words about that time:

"Doubts, questions and fears marked the passing of long hours. Where was God? The walls echoed back the barren question. Turmoils wrestled within. Was such a demand on God impertinence? Ahead loomed an apparently dead-end street... Days of fasting, still there was no answer... Two months passed—an eternity fitted into time. Not a breeze stirred in the spiritual world, not even a tiny cloud the size of a man's hand appeared..."[5]

"When I Wish, I Can Bring Them In"

After two months of "dry" prayer, Dr. Miller gave in to an impulse to "set God a date," or ultimatum, and he told the Lord that after that time he would return to "missionary business as usual." The very day the set period ended, Dr. Miller prepared to set out with his pocketful of tracts as he had promised, but God sent a frustrated missionary and his unsaved teenage son to Miller's door. Hours passed as the missionary poured out his heart and all hope of a day spent in "visitation" disappeared. As the two visitors prepared to leave, Miller asked the youth some searching questions, and the boy's heart suddenly broke as the Spirit of God brought him to repentance. Afterward, the Lord told Dr. Miller something that every believer should hear. He said, "You see, son, when I wish I can bring them in. Now return to prayer until I tell you it is time to leave."[6]

We don't fast and pray simply to move God's hand. We do it because we want to enter into relationship with Him. Months later, God spoke again to Dr. Miller. I'll never forget the way he described the moment the Holy Spirit finally moved in. He said, "It was like sitting at the bottom of a river of golden honey." When I asked him why he described it as honey instead of water, he said, "Because it was so sweet, so pure, and so satisfying that only using the description of the honey would have been adequate."

When God spoke to Miller, it was to give him specific instructions about a prayer meeting he was to establish. The missionary wasn't too excited about the idea because every attempt to interest his few Argentine followers in prayer had failed up to that point. To make things worse, God told him to tell the people that the meeting would go on every night from 8:00 p.m. until midnight. And if the people weren't willing to pray the entire four-hour period, they should stay home! When Miller walked into the church building to pray, the only people willing to pray with him were a timid young servant girl and a backslidden man and his young wife. Dr. Miller told me that every night they prayed it was "dead." Nothing happened. Most of us would say, "We must have missed God. Let's go eat."

It Would Be Too Foolish!

Every night after prayer, Dr. Miller would ask his prayer partners one by one, "Did any one of you receive an impulse from God, something that He wants you to do? Did you get a song that we need to sing? Should we pray aloud—anything at all?" One night everyone said no except the young wife. She admitted that she had sensed a strange urge to walk to the table in the center of the room and hit it, but she quickly dismissed it, saying, "Oh, it would be too foolish." At 11:00 p.m. three days later, Miller finally convinced the young woman to act on her leading, but only after everyone else had stood and struck the table first. When she hit the table, Miller said:

> "Immediately a rushing wind swept into the room from the southeast corner. In seconds, the retiring, timid servant lass was on her feet worshipping the Lord in great ecstasy, her hands raised in the air. Her face was transformed, radiating the joy and glory of the Lord as she spoke in an unknown tongue. The backslidden, rebellious man who had consistently resisted the call of God over his life fell under the table and there began to worship the Lord in another tongue as the Spirit gave utterance. His young

wife...cried out, 'I, too, Lord!'...and she too broke forth in a strange tongue."[7]

Something happened in the heavenlies that night in early June of 1949, when that young woman finally obeyed God and struck the table. In the months and years after her simple act of obedience released the Presence of God, people began to respond so freely to the gospel that Dr. Miller set up a Bible Institute in City Bell, a city just outside of Buenos Aires, to train Argentine workers for the Kingdom.

In June 1951, an angel appeared to a Polish student named Alexander who had come from the deep forests of Argentina to attend Dr. Miller's Bible Institute. This young man, who had once been a gang leader and troublemaker, had experienced a miraculous encounter with God in one of Dr. Miller's meetings in his small community of Chaco. He had become a young man of prayer, and he excused himself from his fellow students and stole away to pray in the woods late one night, when an angel suddenly appeared to him. The Presence of the Lord was so strong and Alexander was so frightened that he ran back to the Institute where all the resident students were now sleeping, and he began to pound on the door.

When someone finally got up and opened the door, Alexander ran inside, and the angelic visitor, along with the overpowering Presence of the Lord, went right into the building with him! In moments, all the other young people were wide awake and crying out to God in repentance. That night, and for many nights afterward, the students were afraid to be alone in the Presence—God began to deal with every single one of them. During this time Dr. Miller announced that all classes would be suspended, to be replaced by a time of prayer.

The Cry That Originates From God

Only a few moments after the group of 50 Argentine students and missionary-teachers began to pray on the morning of June 5, 1951, the angelic visitor returned to stand beside young Alexander again. Then he took him up into an open vision and took him to "visit" all the nations and cities that the Lord had marked to touch with His glory before His coming. (They didn't know it then, but the angel would come a total of 50 times, and each time leave a heavenly message with them.) They failed to write down the many locations given that day because Alexander's vision and his vocal recitation of the cities and nations continued unbroken for hours. Taking note of all he said was made even more complicated by the fact that Alexander named these places in their native tongues!

"[Alexander] opened his lips and began to speak, slowly, deliberately, distinctly, repeating each word twice or more, telling us the name of each city he visited.

"Cities. City after city. Beginning with cities in Argentina, he then moved out from country to country just as if he was deliberately reading off the names from an atlas. Neither student nor traveller could have named such a long list, much less this lad from the forest jungles of Chaco with barely a primary school education.

"As he moved in spirit from country to country, he gave the names of each city in the language of the country, English, German, Slavic, Arabic, and languages he didn't know."[8]

Dr. Miller specifically remembers hearing Alexander mention Toronto, Ontario, in Canada and Pittsburgh, Pennsylvania. The same thing happened the next day, but this time Alexander spoke in an unknown tongue, and God used a young man named Celsio, who was even less educated than Alexander, to interpret by the Spirit. He was so choked up in his fear and awe over the messages that he had to write out every word of the interpretations. Dr. Miller said they soon realized that God wanted the messages written down so they wouldn't be lost or forgotten.

Every day the Presence of the Lord was so strong among them that most of the people present could do nothing but weep. Dr. Miller said, "For ten weeks the Spirit of God moved on us in horrific conviction of sin and repentance. It was something we couldn't turn on or turn off." Sometimes the students and missionaries wept so much that streams of tears would flow across the unpainted brick floor to form puddles. It was nothing to see people sprawled face down on the hard floor unmoving except for their convulsive weeping for four hours or more at a time. "I wouldn't have believed it possible for human beings to shed so many tears," Dr. Miller said. The students began to denounce all the works of the world and the flesh, and they totally rejected the rulership of satan in their lives and nation.

"Because the power and presence of God made the very grounds around a vortex of spiritual activity, we did not sit around reading and meditating upon the Angelic messages during those months. The Presence of God was too real—the work of the Spirit in our own heart too vital—the Bible too important a book to make the prophecies a center. The Lord Himself was our center. Prayer became a strong, terrible crying out to God... Among the many visions, messages and divers manifestations, the most important were the deep, heart-tearing intercessions when our very souls were poured out before the Lord in a cry that originated in God Himself."[9]

The angelic visitations and prayer continued for four months, but the period of heart-wrenching repentance and weeping began to end after about 10 weeks. Dr. Miller told me that in September of 1951, the Lord spoke prophetically to the intercessors at City Bell, saying, "Weep no more. The Lion of the tribe of Judah has roared over Argentina. The ruling powers and principalities have been cast down, and you have an open heaven. *Because I have found 50 righteous Argentines* who would renounce the world, the flesh, and the rulership of satan, you have an open heaven." (Dr. Miller explained that this gave God a "judicial right" according to His own laws to claim all of Argentina. This may well be linked to God's statement to Abraham concerning the wicked city of Sodom in Genesis 18:26. Argentina was the only nation redeemed in this manner in all of Dr. Miller's extensive travels and ministry among the nations of the world over the past 50 years.) If it is a principle, and if it only took 50 righteous people for God to claim Argentina from satan, how many would it take for the United States, or England, or Germany, or Japan?

When God Lifts the Burden

Everyone felt as if a great weight had been taken from their shoulders. Dr. Miller said that after they received that prophetic word from God, none of them wept anymore. "It was impossible to even make them weep," Dr. Miller said. "The spirit of weeping lifted because the repentance and cleansing was complete. God's work in that area was finished. When it's God, it's God. You can't hardly pray over something when the Lord lifts the burden."

When Dr. Miller and the students and missionary-teachers finally emerged from prayer, they were surprised to hear that an unsuccessful coup had taken place that very day. Even though the coup failed to unseat the Peron government, they knew that God's prophetic warning, that He was going to shake the government, was coming to pass. One of those things concerned Evita Peron, the second wife of Argentine President Juan Peron.

Evita Peron: The Rest of the Story

Broadway musicals and major motion pictures have glamorized Evita Peron in countless ways, and she was a beautiful and accomplished woman of immense popularity and political power. Unfortunately, Evita was also deeply involved in spiritism (the practice of communicating with familiar spirits claiming to be the spirits of the dead) and the occult, and she openly flaunted it. Dr. Miller told me that she had already conducted a major national conference on spiritism and was planning another one. The Lord spoke prophetically that because she was leading the people into witchcraft and the occult, "...Evita Peron shall tremble. She will be removed...she will see the thunder of My Presence fall on her heart. She will tremble for she shall see Me just as I Am. She will scream, pull out her hair, and cry out in anger, but to no avail. She will still die." The Lord would cause her to tremble, even as she had made men tremble.

Dr. Miller said that by that time Evita had usurped more dictatorial power than her husband had.[10]

At approximately the same time that the sense of release came to the prayer warriors at the Bible school, Evita Peron was forced by the military to suddenly withdraw her bid to run as vice president of Argentina alongside her husband. Had she been elected to that office, all power would have been consolidated between the Perons alone. One month later, her cancerous uterus was removed, but her condition was still diagnosed as terminal. Numerous trips to top hospitals in New York City and elsewhere didn't help her, nor did the best efforts of her spiritist friends and counselors. The seed of Evita's destruction came to full term nine months later when she died an agonizing death on July 26, 1952, at the age of 33. It is said that Evita died ripping out her beautiful hair because of her rage and the pain and agony that she experienced.

According to Dr. Miller, God had also said that He would remove every person whom Evita had placed in the Argentine government. Over the next 12 months, every single person Evita had put into government positions died. The last one was Evita's own brother, who was killed in a shootout in Uruguay.

God Sends a Mere Man

Late in 1951, possibly at the same time the students in Argentina felt a release in the heavens, God spoke to a little known American healing evangelist named Tommy Hicks and said, "I want you to go to Argentina and pray for a man named Peron." Dr. Miller told me that over lunch many years later, Demos Shakarian, the founder of Full Gospel

Business Men's Fellowship International (FGBMFI) told him that Tommy Hicks was a guest in his Los Angeles, California, home at the time.

Demos (who went to be with the Lord in 1993 at the age of 80) said that he and his wife, Rose, received a vision of FGBMFI and of how to organize it late that night. As the couple walked down the hall of their home talking about the vision they'd received, they noticed light coming under the door of their guest's room despite the late hour. When they talked with Tommy Hicks, he told them he too had received a vision and a command to "go to Argentina and pray for Peron." He told Demos and Rose that he didn't recognize the name of Peron.[11]

During Tommy Hicks' flight to Argentina in 1954, he asked one of the Argentine stewardesses, "Do you know anyone by the name of Peron?" She said, "Why yes, I think we do. That is our president's name." This was three years after God spoke to Tommy about Argentina in the Shakarians' home, as well as after the Lord had spoken again to Hicks about the country while he ministered in Oklahoma. In late 1953, a small committee of evangelical Pentecostal leaders in Argentina known to Dr. Miller contacted Tommy Hicks about conducting a "mass evangelism crusade" in their country. (Tommy wasn't their "first" choice. They had already contacted T.L. and Daisy Osborne about the crusade, but they were already committed to a healing and evangelistic crusade in Chile at the time.) The only choice God left to the committee was this unknown American healing evangelist named Hicks. To make matters worse, Hicks wanted them to rent a large soccer stadium that would hold 25,000 people. The committee members were used to ministering in Argentina with only small successes at a time. Their faith could barely conceive of renting a 2,500-seat auditorium, and they knew it would take presidential approval to rent the city's soccer stadium. The committee protested, "The obstacles are too great! It has never been done before! How will we fill it!"

When Tommy Hicks suggested to the committee that they request a personal interview for him with the president of Argentina, the leaders said, "It is impossible!" However, Tommy Hicks knew he had heard from God, and he had made a commitment to obey Him.

Tommy Hicks told Dr. Miller later on that he left that discouraging meeting and went to his hotel room to pray. He knew that God was greater than any dictator or bureaucracy, but he had been told that even high foreign government officials had been turned away by Peron. Why would he want to see an unknown "Americano" preacher? In the end, Tommy's faith in God came out on top, and the humble preacher from Lancaster, California, turned up at the gate of the "Rose House" (the Argentine equivalent of the White House in the United States) that very afternoon.

Hicks was stopped by a stern guard who curtly said, "Who are you? What do you want?" When Hicks answered, "I want to see the president," the guard raised his eyebrow and asked, "Why in the world would you want to see President Peron?" Without blinking an eye, Hicks said, "I want permission to rent a large stadium in town so I can preach the gospel and pray for the sick." The guard shook his head and said, "Are you crazy? Do you really believe that God still heals today?" and Tommy said, "Yes, He can and He will!"

Will God Heal Me?

"Well, as a matter of fact, I have a physical condition that I've shown to doctors, but I can't get any relief from it. Will God heal me?" the guard asked. Tommy Hicks didn't answer the question; he just said, "Give me your hand," and he prayed the prayer of faith right there on the street. The power of God flooded the man's body and removed every trace of his pain and sickness! The amazed guard told Hicks, "Come back tomorrow and I will get you in to see President Peron."

When Hicks returned the next day, he and his interpreter were ushered directly into Juan Peron's office. The governor of Mendosa was in the President's office that day when the two men entered the room, and Hicks told Dr. Miller what happened next. After President Peron politely greeted his guests, he motioned to them to sit down and asked why they wanted to see him. Tommy Hicks didn't hesitate a moment. He said, "I want to hold a citywide salvation and healing campaign in a large stadium, with full press and radio coverage." As President Peron listened thoughtfully, Tommy went on to present the gospel to him as well.

Then President Peron asked, "Can God can heal me?" Juan Peron was suffering from an incurable and disfiguring skin condition at the time. The condition had become so extensive since the death of his wife, Evita Peron, two years earlier, that he had banned all photographs and refused to go out in public anymore, even though his skin condition had become common knowledge. Without hesitation, Tommy Hicks said, "Give me your hand." With their hands clasped over President Juan Peron's desk, Tommy prayed the prayer of faith, and the power of God flowed into Peron's body.

Everyone in the room saw President Peron's skin become as clean and fresh as a baby's, and the leader stepped back in amazement and exclaimed, *"Dios mio, estoy curado!"* ("My God, I am cured!")[12]

President Peron gave Tommy Hicks everything he wanted, and God made the impossible possible. Peron was overthrown in a military coup a year later, but he was able to rewrite many Argentine laws that are still in effect today that protect freedom of religion and religious expression. By faith, Tommy Hicks preached the gospel and prayed for the sick for 62 days—from mid-April to mid-June in 1954—in Buenos Aires. The governor of Mendosa who first met Brother Hicks in President Peron's office brought his ailing wife to the meetings and was able to see the Lord raise her up, totally healed of heart problems.

The 25,000-seat Atlantic soccer stadium quickly proved to be too small for the crowds that flocked to the crusade, and Hicks moved the meetings to the 180,000-seat Huracan bullfighting stadium. This facility had never been filled to capacity since it was built, but upwards of 200,000 people descended upon the stadium day and night, and traffic was snarled in every direction as thousands of people streamed to the healing crusade from throughout Argentina and South America. Untold thousands of people were saved, healed, and delivered. Between three to six million people attended the meetings, and ushers were literally working 12-hour shifts in futile attempts to keep up with the press of people seeking God's touch.

God had opened the heavens over Argentina. In Dr. Miller's words, "Heaven bent low and kissed earth."[13] Tommy Hicks knew his strength and endurance were gone after two months of unending ministry with little or no breaks for sleep or meals. He finally boarded a plane for the United States in mid-June while thousands of grateful Argentines waved and cheered in the rain. This was literally three years after God had opened the heavens in answer to the intercession and vicarious repentance on behalf of their nation of heartbroken Bible school students just outside of Buenos Aires.

Revival and miracles are still occurring in Argentina, and I believe that is the source of much of the anointing that we have today in the revival and renewal currently sweeping across the earth. It is highly likely that even the fire of the Argentine revival of 1954 could be traced back to the fiery anointing God brought to Topeka, Kansas, and Azusa Street at the turn of the century. Perhaps it can all be traced back to Pentecost in the Book of Acts because there is only one Holy Spirit.

This is interaction between God and man, between believers and churches of many nations. This "Body life" and spiritual *cross-pollination* is the heart of God for the Church today! Cross-pollination refers to "the transfer of pollen from one flower to the stigma of another" according to *Merriam-Webster's Collegiate Dictionary.*[14] In the spirit realm, it refers to *the transfer of heavenly deposits of God's glory and anointing from one believer to another and from one group of believers in a locale to those in another.* This supernatural interaction openly displays the supernatural nature of the Church and the Kingdom of God. Paul wrote:

> *I planted, Apollos watered, but God gave the increase. So then neither he who plants is anything, nor he who waters, but God who gives the increase.*

Now he who plants and he who waters are one, and each one will receive his own reward according to his own labor. For we are God's fellow workers; you are God's field, you are God's building. According to the grace of God which was given to me, as a wise master builder I have laid the foundation, and another builds on it. But let each one take heed how he builds on it (1 Corinthians 3:6-10).

Dr. Edward Miller *sowed* alone on his knees in prayer for months. The 50 Argentines *watered* with their tears and heartbroken repentance on behalf of their nation. Tommy Hicks, himself a fervent man of prayer, *reaped* the harvest for God in the fullness of time. All were moved and empowered by God, but no one was sufficient for the task in and of themselves. It was *God's doing* from beginning to end, and we are still reaping the benefits today, more than four decades later. This is the economy of God displayed in all its glory.

We Are All Kings and Priests

In Tommy Hicks' vision from 1961, he saw a little lady in a gingham dress go in and empty out a mental institution. This picture illustrated that God will do a new thing in the last days because He will use "average people," persons whose only credentials are their relationship with Him. That is why repentance and reconciliation are the chief messages of this great revival and harvest today. That is why intercession has suddenly become so important to people who once avoided the subject like the plague. That is why holiness is being preached so strongly today. God wants His people to come into right relationship with Him so that we can all function as priests and ministers before Him.

God Is Calling Us to the Mountain

God has always wanted a *nation* of priests, not just a select, elite few. God told the Israelites, "And you shall be to Me a kingdom of priests and a holy nation" (Ex. 19:6a). But in the next chapter, the people gave in to their fears and refused to draw near to God: They were afraid because they had not obeyed God and *sanctified* (or set apart) themselves according to the same standards set by Moses and the priests. Given that fact, they had good reason to fear, but it cost them their destiny as a kingdom of priests. They decided it was better to have someone *else* hear God for them.

Much of the Church is still in the same, miserable place today, even though Jesus died on the cross to cleanse us from sin and shame. It is time for all of us to draw near to God. He's not just calling a "Moses" to His mountain today; He is calling every one of us to come close to Him. He is calling each of us to join Him in His greatest redemptive work since He died on the cross—*as intercessors.*

I've shared the Argentina stories with you for a very specific reason: They reveal God's blueprint for revival in the earth. First, He works on a few who are willing to obey, even in the face of the impossible. These early pioneers, in turn, break through and bring a few more into God's glory and purposes. When this newly formed band of believers lay down their own agendas, preconceived ideas, and limitations and in absolute obedience begin to *pray, intercede*, and *worship* God in the Spirit, God then opens the heavens over their homes, churches, cities, and nations. That is when true revival will sweep across nations and people. And that is what God wants to do in you and I today!

Endnotes

1.   Excerpted from the prophecy by Tommy Hicks in Charles and Frances Hunter, *To Heal the Sick* (Kingwood, Texas: Hunter Books, n.d.), 8-16.

2.   Dr. R. Edward Miller, *Cry for Me Argentina* (Fairburn, Georgia: Peniel Publications, n.d.), 5-6.

3.   Miller, *Cry for Me*, 21.

4.   Miller, *Cry for Me*, 21.

5.   Miller, *Cry for Me*, 23.

6.   Miller, *Cry for Me*, 24.

7.   Miller, *Cry for Me*, 27-28.

8.   Miller, *Cry for Me*, 12-13.

9.   Miller, *Cry for Me*, 15,17.

10.   Miller, *Cry for Me*, 18.

11.   It is my understanding that the Shakarians actually financed some of the costs of Tommy's trip to Argentina three years later. The Shakarians were very successful in business and never took a salary from Full Gospel Businessmen's Fellowship International. They founded the organization in 1952 to reach the business community for Christ, and they directed the organization for four decades. Their son, Richard, who now serves as International President of FGBMFI, served on the staff of Tommy Hicks' ministry, Manifest Deliverance and Worldwide Evangelism, Inc., for several years.

12.   Miller, *Cry for Me*, 40-41. (Narrative and information from these pages of the book is supplemented with

information received directly from Dr. Miller by phone at the time of this writing early in 1998.)

13. Miller, *Cry for Me*, 47.

14. *Merriam-Webster's Collegiate Dictionary*, 10th ed. (Springfield, Massachusetts: Merriam-Webster, Inc., 1994), *pollination*, 278.

Chapter 2

The Bees and the Giants

So I have come down to deliver them out of the hand of the Egyptians, and to bring them up from that land to a good and large land, to a land flowing with milk and honey... (Exodus 3:8).

Thousands of years ago, God made an ancient promise to Moses concerning the Jews enslaved in Egypt. Since that day, that promise has been quoted and proclaimed time and again as a symbol of God's delivering and saving power, and for good reason. God said that He had *heard their cries*, and in response to their prayers, He would lead them to a good land, a large land, a land flowing with milk (milk is only available where cows, sheep, or goats can thrive on abundant feed grains and grasses in peace and stability). It was also promised to be a land flowing with *honey*. Hold that thought a moment, and look at this rarely quoted Messianic prophecy in the Book of Isaiah:

Therefore the Lord Himself will give you a sign: Behold, the virgin shall conceive and bear a Son, and

shall call His name Immanuel. **Curds and honey He
shall eat,** *that He may* **know to refuse the evil and
choose the good** (Isaiah 7:14-15).

Do you get the feeling that honey is somehow related to
discernment and obedience? God is bringing the Church
into a land that is flowing with milk and honey, and we are
at the edge of our "river Jordan." We don't want to be like
the Israelites who, when they looked across the river Jordan
at their land of promise for the first time, failed to enter in
because of their unbelief and their rebellion.

John the Baptist ate locusts and honey, according to
Mark 1:6. What was his ministry? Repentance. So somehow
the honey message has to do with repentance, discernment,
taking it into the land, and a witness. God is pouring out His
Spirit upon the Church today. Who can contain it without
using it to build up themselves? God wants to do more than
we could ever imagine, and He wants to use every one of us
in the process. If we limit Him, we also limit what He can
do in our lives.

A Church After God's Own Heart

The Lord is drawing His Body into a new level and new
place with Him. Where we've been before hasn't gotten the
job done. I believe that, in the days ahead, we will look on our
accomplishments and meetings of the past as a vague, unim-
portant memory in comparison to the new things He will
bring to us—as long as the Church continues its walk into
repentance, holiness, and absolute abandon to God's plan for
the future. He will begin to come into our meetings and "cap-
ture our hearts," and it will be nothing to see worship last for
hours. David and Solomon had continual 24-hour worship

in their services. Why do you think that David was called "a man after God's own heart" (see 1 Sam. 13:14)? David had a lot of problems, just like all the rest of us, but he was set apart from other men because he was a man of worship. He learned how to enter into the Presence of God through the courts of praise and into the arena of worship. It is time for the Church to catch on to David's secret.

> *After this I will return and will rebuild the tabernacle of David, which has fallen down; I will rebuild its ruins, and I will set it up; so that the rest of mankind may seek the Lord, even all the Gentiles who are called by My name, says the Lord who does all these things* (Acts 15:16-17).

James quoted these words taken from Amos 9:11 to provide scriptural proof that God had begun to fulfill that very prophecy through the ministry of Paul and Barnabas among the Gentiles. That work is picking up even more momentum in our day! God is not rebuilding the tabernacle of Moses; He is rebuilding David's tabernacle. Why? Because He is restoring the continuous worship and intimate relationships characterized by David's tabernacle, and later by Solomon's temple. Solomon had obvious flaws and failures, but in his early reign, he called for 24-hour-a-day worship and praise to the Lord.

We are on the verge of a harvest of souls that will be greater than anything we have ever imagined. We are thrilled with the number of people who have come to Jesus Christ at the altars in Brownsville and in the revivals in South America, but these salvations are just a drop in the bucket. There are billions of people who haven't heard the gospel or been brought to the cross of Christ. We have a lot of work ahead of us, but it will only get done when we adopt a "Kingdom mentality." We need to get away from our traditional "us four and no more" way of thinking. Our vision must be much bigger. Many who come here to the revival in Brownsville just want revival in their church. We need to see that God wants to shake every single nation on the earth in this spiritual awakening and shaking. Wherever I go, I am finding wonderful people who represent the embryo of revival in their nations and cities. It is just the beginning.

The Lord has shown me that the most important thing about this revival, or worldwide awakening, is the unity of the brethren. We must have unity—not only between denominations but between cultures and nationalities as well. The outworking of this unity—the "verb" that goes with the "noun"—is cross-pollination, cooperation, or interaction as an organism, if you will.

We also face a strong temptation to stop our forward movement in God at some point and begin to draw inward to create a denomination to memorialize what God is doing. This has happened every single time there has been a great move of God. Each time, the believers became "internalized," or turned inward, away from further change and harvest. The only way to "make camp" is to *stop progress*. Once they "camped out" or stopped to build a theological monument, they "died" there because God didn't stop His movement to accomplish His purposes.

Ford the Water, Face the Giants

The promised land of Canaan looked good to the Israelites as they stood on the banks of the muddy Jordan, but they still didn't cross the river to possess the land God had for them. Most refused because of fear and unbelief. Others refused because they thought that the land on the wilderness side of the Jordan "looked real good" too. Camping out on the border of your dream and divine calling will never bring you into the whole promises of God! Nothing of value comes without a leap of faith in the face of fear. The Lord wants to bring the Church into the full promises of God, but the only way it will happen is for us to ford the waters and face the giants—"Ya gotta believe to receive."

During a recent visit to Israel, I visited Ruth Ward Heflin's Mount Zion Fellowship in Jerusalem. Ruth wrote the landmark book entitled *Glory*, in which she described the higher levels of intercession with its dancing, singing, worship, and praise that lead to "the glory." I went there specifically to worship the Lord with her, and believe me, everyone there had a good time. We danced, sang, did circle dances, and, of course, interceded to the Lord.

I've always been free with my hands because I understand the Old Testament teaching about priestly service to God, including the "wave offering" that the priests were to offer to God. Many of the intercessors in that meeting were making different hand movements during worship, so Ruth asked everyone, "What was the Lord showing you while we were dancing and worshiping?" One by one they began to share that they felt like they were "planting a harvest." Some of them said they felt like they were reaping the harvest using ancient harvesting scythes.

The Workers Are Coming!

Meanwhile I was thinking, *Lila, you are getting weirder and weirder all the time. What in the world were you doing?* I was concerned because my movements took on a totally new twist. I was moving my hands as if tossing something upward and blowing. Then it came to my spirit that I was "pollinating" the fields, because everything that we were doing that day had to do with the harvest. This didn't totally connect until one night when I was driving to a revival meeting at Brownsville Assembly of God; all of a sudden the understanding came into my mind. Now this was in the spring of 1996, just when we were beginning to see people come in to Brownsille from greater distances.

I thought, *That's it! The Lord is telling me, "The workers are coming." These "worker bees" are gathering the pollen. This is why we are beginning to see pastors, prayer workers, and leaders coming in from different states; they are gathering the pollen from Brownsville and they are taking it back to their own "hives." I was dancing a prophetic dance while in Jerusalem—the dance of the honeybee worker who gives detailed directions to the other bees in the hive about a rich harvest of pollen so that they may collect and create more honey.*

Since that day, the heart of my ministry has been "cross-pollination," because God has shown me that is *His heart*! So I'm really not offended or bothered by my "bee lady" nickname. Again, I understand that the metaphor of the honeybee and the beehive is a limited metaphor, but it is a parable from the Lord that reveals His purposes for today. God is sending people to Brownsville (and to other places such as Toronto Airport Christian Fellowship, Holy Trinity

Brompton Anglican Church in London, and Ken Gott's Revival Now! Ministries in Sunderland, England—just to name a very few) from their own fellowships and churches (their "hives," if you will). Two things happen when these "worker bees" visit renewal and revival sites—they deposit their own pollen in these "hot spots" and they take home the pollen, or glory, that God deposited in these locations. In other words, God is cross-pollinating His Church with glory!

In the spirit realm, as in the natural, cross-pollination produces much more strength in the harvest and causes it to be much more fruitful than if each "flower" was dependent on one "bee" or "hive" alone. As I reflected on what God had shown me, I shared it with Brenda Kilpatrick, the wife of Pastor John Kilpatrick at Brownsville Assembly of God. Brenda is an anointed minister and intercessor in her own right, and she told me that an evangelist named Dale Van Steenis had come to Brownsville before the revival, even before construction on the current auditorium had been completed, and had given a very strong prophecy related to this vision.

I Saw Honey Dripping...

The Lord said through Brother Van Steenis, "Make the foundation strong. Have everything point upward toward Christ, and *He will bring the workers*." Now, that was several years before the Holy Spirit showed up on Father's Day, 1995. After the outpouring of the Holy Spirit began at Brownsville Assembly, Dale Van Steenis called Pastor Kilpatrick and told him the rest of the prophecy. He also recently shared the story of the vision to the Brownsville congregation. In those pre-revival days, Van Steenis had been asked to handle Sunday evening service for the Kilpatricks, who had been called to look after an urgent matter out of town. He was sitting in the church van and glancing toward the partially finished auditorium structure just before the evening service, when the sun rose in an open vision:

"...the rays [of the sun] came down on the sloped roof of this building [the Brownsville Assembly auditorium] from the sunlight that was shining all over it, and when they came to the eaves...the rays of the sun turned into honey and began to drip off the eaves and all the way around this building. I have been to this church a number of times and I know this campus, and as far as you could see down all these streets people were coming. They were coming shackled, they were coming drug addicted, coming in wheelchairs, they were coming in chains, and as soon as they came and touched their lips to that honey all the bondage flew off of them and they began to rejoice...

"I was caused to understand I should just secret that in my heart, and for a number of years I did. Finally, years later, I told the Pastor [Kilpatrick], but for that night I was to leave that issue alone. But I said that night, 'Lord, I would feel a lot better going into that service if You'd just let me know what You plan with this.' And He said, 'I am going to command My glory on that building, and people will come from all over the world that are bound and sick, depressed and weary, and they will touch the sweetness of the Lord in that place and will recover their health.' How many know two and a half years later the honeycomb is still full and it's still sweet."[1]

This sounded really strange, but once we began to understand more about bees and their habits, we began to identify the honey and the "workers" with the ministry of intercessors. When Brenda Kilpatrick and I talked about "cross-pollination" in 1996, you need to realize that we shared a traditional (if you can call it that) understanding of intercession. I was familiar with the "stock and trade" tools of spiritual warfare. I knew about our authority in Christ to bind and loose things in the spirit realm so that they will be bound on earth. I also knew about the "spiritual mapping" or charting techniques used in South America and written about by Dr. C. Peter Wagner of Fuller Theological Seminary. But God issued a challenge to us when we decided to let God be God and do whatever He wanted to do with us in prayer. That was when He said to me:

"If you will be like children, I will take you places that you've never been to. You will see things that you've never seen. You will do things that you've never done, and hear things that you've never heard before."

We said, "We are going to be like children," and we began to have full liberty in our intercessory prayer rooms. One of the first things that God began to show us was how He wanted to use dance in prophetic intercession. We couldn't figure it out at first, but we did it anyway because it felt like the right thing to do. (Frankly, it was totally against everything I had ever been taught or believed. My emphasis had always been on "the integrity of the Word." If you could show me in the Word with five witnesses confirming it, then I might do it. In other words, I wasn't exactly spontaneous by nature.)

Then we began to dance in circles spontaneously under the direction of the Holy Spirit (at the time we didn't know that this is a key component of Jewish culture in general, and of Messianic Jewish worship in particular). We were "green recruits" in the Lord's supernatural school of prayer, drawn straight from the traditional church. We knew something was up when we started dancing "figure eights" and doing other "strange" things at the Lord's leading. That was when I began to discover some fascinating facts about bees that helped me understand what the Lord was doing with us. I read Bobbie Jean Merck's article entitled, "Fanner Bees & Porters" in *A Great Love Overflow* magazine published by the ministry of the same name, and her insights really began to open my spiritual eyes:

> "Those who have knowledge of bees understand the work of 'fanner bees.' These are the bees in hives that fan the air so rapidly with their wings that their movements appear as a fine mist.

> "As they fan their wings, they are pulling clean, pure air into the hive and pushing unclean, foul air out of the hive, and this enables the other bees to do their assigned work in the proper atmosphere.

> "Intercessors can be likened to these 'fanner bees.' The intercessors' assignment is to pull the clean, pure breath of God—the manifestation of the Holy Spirit—into the Church. This assignment includes pushing out the unclean, foul atmosphere. This they do in the prayer closet."[2]

I have since found this old English story that describes the work of "fanner bees":

A Parable of the Fanner Bees

It was a glorious night of mid-summer—a moon at full and a host of stars. The old bee-garden was bathed in soft crystalline light—and ever so light a breeze lisped in the tree-tops. At the door of one of the hives we came to a halt. There arose from the hive a sibilant note...persistent...not unlike the sound of sea-waves...advancing...retreating.

"They are Fanner-bees," whispered the old bee-keeper. "It's their job to keep the hive sweet and fresh. They're standing with their heads lowered, turned toward the center of the hive. Their wings are moving so rapidly that if you saw them you would think you were looking at a gray mist. They are drawing the bad air through one side of the entrance, whilst the pure air is sucked in on the other side."

Standing there close to nature, listening to the bee fanners, I felt close to one of nature's wonders, the mystery of the hive life. Presently the old bee-keeper stooped to the hive, holding a lighted candle in his hand. Instantly the light was extinguished by the strong air current, those infinitesimal bee wings, moving in unison, making a draft so strong that the candle light was instantly quenched. Think of it!

As we stood there in the star-lit garden, the old preacher said, "The Fanners—drawing out the bad air, letting in the fresh. Isn't that how people who call themselves Christians ought to act?" If we had enough fanners, if they were as keen on their jobs as those bees were on theirs, wouldn't the great hive of the world grow sweet and fresh?[3]

One woman told me that she had felt led to start praying "for the worker bees to come in," and she wanted to know the significance of "worker bees." I told her the Spirit was having her ask for intercessors to come in. The truth of the matter is that every member of the Body of Christ is called to intercession because it is part of the "priesthood of the believer."

This reminds me of another fascinating fact about bees. Each worker bee functions in virtually every responsibility in the hive in its 40-day lifetime. Its first responsibility on day one is to clean out the wax cell from which it just emerged. Then it helps keep the other young members of the brood warm, feeds the larvae, produces wax for the hive, and helps build the comb and carry food. At mid-life, the bee will assume guard duty for the hive until, at the age of 22 days, it begins to fly from the hive collecting pollen, nectar, and water. Intercessors are worker bees who will come in and help build the hive to God's glory.[4]

My purpose is not to give you a definitive lesson on bees or beekeeping, but I want you to see an important principle in the spirit realm: *The most important function of intercession in the local church is to maintain and to draw "what God is doing" into other levels.* This sounds strange, I know, but I'm afraid that the bizarre antics of the Old Testament prophets just wouldn't have passed the grade with the critics we have today who are constantly saying, "This couldn't be God because it doesn't look like Sunday morning in *my church*!" Yet many of these same critics like to sing, "Every promise in the Book is mine..." forgetting that the "promises" in the Book were transmitted through some very strange people who did some very strange things at God's command! Ezekiel and Hosea did some very bizarre things. Going back to our illustration, the fanner bees were in charge of bringing fresh oxygen into the hives while driving out all the bad air and regulating the internal temperature of the hive.

The biblical importance of "body ministry" is also reflected in the community life of a beehive. It seems that the entire hive knows when an individual worker bee is missing, because every bee leaves its own unique enzyme or pheromone in the honey when it deposits pollen or processes the pollen into honey. If something happens in the hive and one of the members or workers is gone or out of order, a "moan" or frequency goes through the entire hive, and the workers begin to move around and adjust until that missing place is filled. Every one of us is important in the Body of Christ, and if one of us is missing the remaining members must move to fill the void ("stand in the gap, make up the hedge," see Ezekiel 22:30), so the purposes of God can be fulfilled. If you have ever entered into intercession by the direction of the Holy Spirit, then you know what it is to moan and groan with "words that cannot be uttered," as the Spirit prays through you for situations, individuals, or even nations that you know nothing about. This may simply mean that things are out of place somewhere in the Body of Christ, and not necessarily in your particular congregation.

Prayer Parables and the Dance

I discovered that when worker bees go out to forage for honey, and find a rich source of pollen, they will go back to the hive and perform an elaborate dance in front of other worker bees from the hive. When I learned this I said, "Thank You, Lord. The mysteries are being solved in my mind," because I finally understood that what we were actually doing with our bodies through dance was allowing the Holy Spirit to speak into the spirit realm through our bodies using a non-verbal language. We call them prayer parables. One of the many biblical precedents for this is found in the story of Elisha the prophet and King Joash of Israel, who was told by the prophet to strike the ground with arrows for victory over his enemies. Because the king only struck the ground three times, he was only given partial victory over Syria (see 2 Kings 13:15-19).

King Joash must have felt silly striking the ground with arrows, because he stopped after only three strikes. The prophet was upset because he knew the king's physical obedience to God's prophetic word would have genuine significance in both the spiritual and natural realms. Dr. Edward Miller's experience with the woman striking the table in Argentina is a modern prayer parable in the same vein that began to revolutionize my understanding of prayer.

I also discovered that worker bees seem to be able to navigate with incredible accuracy using the sun and magnetic reference points to find the honey discovered by other worker bees that went before them. Bees seem to be able to "see" colors, and even into the ultraviolet range of the light spectrum, which allows them to see the sun even when it is obscured by the heaviest of clouds. They also have a built-in sensitivity to magnetic fields that lets them accurately determine magnetic north! These two God-given directional systems allow bees to accurately navigate even on cloudy days.[5] Christians have the indwelling Presence of the Holy Spirit in their hearts and the unchanging "true north" of God's Word, which allows us to accurately find our way even in the midst of a swirling spiritual storm or impossible circumstances.

Meet the Bee Lady

Now these are all allegories or metaphors as I said before, but I've discovered that they are persistent ones. God seems to bring up bees and honey no matter where I go! This happens so much that some people are beginning to call me "the bee lady." I realize that we are not bees, and neither the local church nor the Church universal is a "hive." But I've found that God is speaking to other people in many different places about honey and bees. Brenda Kilpatrick and I found ourselves in Kishinev, Moldova, recently with a group of precious intercessors as a part of a "Hear O Israel" ministry team headed by Jonathan Bernis of Jacksonville, Florida. I started talking about this revelation about bees and honey and an intercessor's eyes suddenly became very big. She said, "As we came into the city of Kishinev, I saw a honeycomb over the whole city with honey dripping down." All I could say was, "Thank You, Jesus! We are going to have some great meetings here. God is going to move mightily!" And He did. They had met stiff resistance all over the area, but when we came to Kishinev, it was just wonderful. We had our normal opposition, but we were able to have our meetings and thousands of people came to know Jesus Christ—and many of them were Jews.

As I write these words, God is moving all across this planet, but we are all of one Spirit, serving one God and one Savior. Each local manifestation of the Spirit may be different, but all are birthed by the one Spirit. We know God is moving in Canada, Argentina, the United States, Great Britain, Australia, New Zealand, Japan, Norway, Finland, and countless other places right now. He wants to "cross-pollinate" His Church with His glory. When I began to study the Argentine revival that was birthed in the 1940's, I kept asking the Lord, "What is the source of this anointing we are enjoying in Pensacola?" And He kept pointing me back to Argentina!

I suppose we could chart the history and see that Evangelist Stephen Hill had been prayed for at Holy Trinity Brompton Anglican Church in London, and prior to that had worked for seven years in the recent Argentine revival with Hector Ferreya. John and Carol Arnott went to Argentina where Claudio Freidzon prayed and laid hands on them the year before the Lord poured out His Spirit on their fellowship in Toronto, Ontario. The list goes on and on. Many times we are too quick to put our stamps of "approval" and "disapproval" on things. We have to avoid saying, "Oh yes, what is going on in Brownsville is good, but I'm not sure about those other places...." It is better to keep our tongues in check and not make any judgments; because if we do, we could very well find ourselves fighting God!

God Moves Wherever He's Welcomed

This move of God is not "a Brownsville thing." It's not an "England thing," and it's not an "Argentine thing." It boils down to this: God is moving wherever He's welcome! If He isn't moving in your church or area yet, He will if He's made welcome. We have to let God be God. Proverbs 14:4 says, "Where no oxen are, the trough is clean; but much increase comes by the strength of an ox." Intercessors are like that, because intercession gets messy. It seems like we're always cleaning up something, but the strength these laborers bring to the Body is almost incalculable.

In Exodus 3:8, God told Moses, "So I have come down to deliver them out of the hand of the Egyptians, and to bring them up from that land to a good and large land, to a land flowing with milk and honey, to the place of the Canaanites and the Hittites and the Amorites and the Perizzites and the Hivites and the Jebusites." God kept His word and delivered the Israelites from Pharaoh's army in the Red Sea. He also wanted to take them into a land flowing with milk and honey, but they wouldn't have it. He even caused them to eat manna, which tasted like honey, as a witness against them that they *could have* entered in (see Ex. 16:31). I believe God is speaking the same word to the Church today if we will only believe and step out in faith to cross the river into His blessing and promised inheritance.

Many Christians think of Cannan land as a mythical place "in the sweet by and by." But when the Jews finally went into the land of Cannan, they still had some literal, physical battles to fight! God didn't hold back either. He told them that once they crossed the river, He wanted *them* to drive out all the *giants*. Yes, He went before them and fought on their behalf, but not until they put on their armor and stepped "in harm's way" solely on the strength of God's promises. In our day, God wants to bring a great deliverance to the Body of Christ. (Yes, some Christians need to be delivered from demonic influences! If you have pastored a church, then you know that all you need to have is one parishioner to be certain of that fact.) He wants to deliver the Church into a season of promise and power marked by His own glory—but only if we will put on our armor and step "into harm's way" solely on the strength of His promises and faithfulness. He wants the Church to step out of the shadows of timidity and fearfulness and openly proclaim Christ to the society of the politically correct and the spiritually dead!

DNA'd With Christ

Frankly, most of us in the Church have been living way beneath our privileges. That may sound shocking or even egotistical to you, but it should sound *biblical* (because it is). Too many of us have been content to be "just as good as the guy next to us or just a little bit better for our ego's sake." Jesus doesn't want us to take the easy way out by measuring ourselves against other people. He made things really tough when He said, "Therefore you shall be perfect, just as your Father in heaven is perfect" (Mt. 5:48). Why would He do such a thing? It is because we are "born again" when we come to Jesus Christ. In that moment, we are "DNA'd with Christ's presence" and His person begins to dwell in our spirit. That means He gives us the possibility of being everything that He is. He wants each of us to be able to honestly say along with the apostle Paul, "Follow me as I follow Christ" (see 1 Cor. 11:1).

God is bringing the Church to a place of accountability. He wants to transform the hidden, apologetic Church (in the "I'm sorry" sense) into the glorious Church of Ephesians 5:27! Our problem is that we have "blended in" all too well. We have been no different than the world, but today God is issuing a clarion call for the Church to come into holiness through repentance. He wants us to exchange our arrogance for humility before Him. He wants us to seek His face rather than His hand. In other words, it's time for the Church to grow up.

It seems like every other month or so, national magazines, newspaper commentators, or television investigative programs in the United States and Europe will do a feature on the faults of "The Couch Potato Generation," or claim that "TV Spectators Make Apathetic Citizens." The concern is valid of course. That same spirit of "spectatorship" has invaded and infected the Church today. People still do not want to be confronted with the living God in all His power and glory because of what it will require of them—especially in the comfort-driven culture of the Western nations.

Protestant churches have developed their own brand of spectator sports by carefully re-creating the priest-centered worship/religion that they so strongly condemn in the liturgical churches. Ask yourself this question, especially if you are a pastor or church leader: Is your local congregation still sitting back and saying, "Let the pastor get the word of the Lord for me, and then I'll do it." If they are, they are lying. The Israelites said the same thing to Moses when they refused to sanctify themselves and approach God on the mountain. No matter how often or how skillfully Moses, or any modern-day preacher, brings a true word of the Lord to his congregation, it is almost certain that the congregation won't do it! God says the "spectator church" is out; the intimate and obedient Church is in. God is calling each of us up to the mountain.

The five years the Church endured just before God began to visit this generation with His Presence were perhaps the most difficult period we've had since the Vietnam War, or perhaps even World War II. God has been maturing Christians through hardships and the pressure they create. To our surprise, most of us are learning that God was in those places years ago, but we just didn't know it. He was getting us ready and cleansing us through tests and trials so that He could dress His Bride—all of us great and small—with His own glory. I know that this isn't a popular teaching, but it's the gospel.

In a related note, I've learned that honeybees, unlike wasps, hornets, and bumblebees, actually "winter over" together. If they die, it isn't because of the cold; it is because they starve to death.[6] (This reminds me of the warning in Amos 8:11: " 'Behold, the days are coming,' says the Lord God, 'That I will send a famine on the land, not a famine of bread, nor a thirst for water, but of hearing the words of the Lord.' ") A beehive can produce as much as 60 pounds of honey per season, but beekeepers will typically harvest only 30 to 40 pounds of honey, leaving the remainder for the bees so they can survive the winter season. Each bee has the capacity to produce body heat as long as it has honey to feed on, and the bees group together in the inner part of the hive during severe weather and will easily survive the winter season—as long as there is honey available to them.[7] In another similarity to a beehive, the Church lives on the honey, God's glory, during the lean years of hardship. But when springtime comes, a glorious harvest is sure to come as well, with more than enough to feed the hive and feed many others besides.

The author of the ultimate "faith" chapter, Hebrews 11, constantly pictured the difficulty of the life of faith alongside God's glory just as the apostle Paul, who said things like, "I have been crucified with Christ; it is no longer I who live, but Christ lives in me; and the life which I now live in the flesh I live by faith in the Son of God, who loved

me and gave Himself for me" (Gal. 2:20). Jesus, the author
and finisher of our faith, said:

> *...If anyone desires to come after Me, let him deny
> himself, and take up his cross daily, and follow Me.
> For whoever desires to save his life will lose it, but
> whoever loses his life for My sake will save it* (Luke
> 9:23-24).

The cross can represent only one thing: our death. The
New Testament is filled with the picture of our "old man"
dying and our "new man" rising in the newness of life. This
is the simple gospel, and God is calling us out of the pew
and into the streets of life to live out our faith among the
people who desperately want to see evidence that God
exists. This generation *wants to believe* that God still has
the power to change the lives of ordinary people. We can
demonstrate this right in front of them, but we must first
meet God's criteria, not ours. He says, "Be holy, for I am
holy" (1 Pet. 1:16b).

The only way that we can take the land or ground God
has promised us is for us to cross the river of fear and face
the inner giants of pride, religiosity, jealousy, unforgiveness, and bitterness. As we go deeper into our promised
land, we may also face the outward giants of religious persecution, ridicule, and demonic opposition of all kinds. It is
wonderful to bask in God's Presence—the fulfillment of the
land of milk and honey for the Church—but there are giants
that will have to be killed.

God told the Israelites to drive out the previous inhabitants of Canaan, but He helped them by allowing hornets to
do it for them. I'm not talking about bees here; I'm talking
about those stinging nuisances that have little else to do.

When we submit to the Father God's tests and trials, He will handle our enemies for us. God is out to reveal a glorious Church to the hurting world, and the world deserves to see Jesus Christ in His Body. So far, the world has seen nothing but bickering, division, backbiting, and competition for man's approval; but God is changing all that. He is raising up an entire army of spiritual "worker bees" anointed to pollinate the harvest fields with His Word, light, and presence, and then to bring in the harvest with unfailing energy and devotion. Scientists have learned that when a field or cash crop is cross-pollinated by a hive of bees, it will produce 25 to 40 percent more than usual! As a result, many farmers will pay beekeepers to bring beehives to their fields and orchards.[8] God is planting holy beehives in the nations of the world for a great harvest, but first, He must transform us.

The Sweet Reward of Obedience

The bottom line is that God has to do the work. Our part is to be willing to trust Him and follow His lead—no matter the cost. There are great rewards for us if we seek Him. Consider some of these incredible promises and the prominence of *honey* in each of them:

> *As an eagle stirs up its nest, hovers over its young, spreading out its wings, taking them up, carrying them on its wings, **so the Lord alone led him**, and there was no foreign god with him. He made him ride in the heights of the earth, that he might eat the produce of the fields; He made him **draw honey from the rock**, and oil from the flinty rock* (Deuteronomy 32:11-13).

*The haters of the Lord would pretend submission to Him, but their fate would endure forever. He would have fed them also with the finest of wheat; and **with honey from the rock I would have satisfied you*** (Psalm 81:15-16).

Consider the role of honey in the life and times of the great prophets of the Bible. Ezekiel encountered honey in the throne room of God!

*Moreover He said to me, "Son of man, eat what you find; eat this scroll, and go, speak to the house of Israel." So I opened my mouth, and He caused me to eat that scroll. And He said to me, "Son of man, feed your belly, and fill your stomach with this scroll that I give you." So I ate, and it was in my mouth **like honey** in sweetness* (Ezekiel 3:1-3).

The scroll was revelation knowledge, and it was like honey in the prophet's mouth. Great revelation knowledge is going to be released in this last day. That is one of the reasons that God is so carefully humbling us and conforming us to the image of Jesus. Even the apostle Paul said he was given a thorn in the flesh because of his abundance of revelation (see 2 Cor. 12:7). The apostle John also encountered honey in his open vision of Heaven received on the Isle of Patmos:

*Then the voice which I heard from heaven spoke to me again and said, "Go, take the little book which is open in the hand of the angel who stands on the sea and on the earth." So I went to the angel and said to him, "Give me the little book." And he said to me, "Take and eat it; and it will make your stomach bitter, but **it will be as sweet as honey** in your mouth." Then I took the little book out of the angel's hand and* *ate it, and **it was as sweet as honey** in my mouth. But when I had eaten it, my stomach became bitter. And he said to me, "You must prophesy again about many peoples, nations, tongues, and kings"* (Revelation 10:8-11).

God is about to release prophecy into the Church at levels we have never known in the past. This, in turn, will help release a tremendous wave of prophetic ministry at every level. One of the principles in God's Word is that everything must first be *spoken out* for it to be confirmed. This principle shows up from Genesis to Revelation. We have changed our intercessory prayer patterns to conform to this God-ordained principle. A long time ago, we abandoned prayer lists in prophetic intercession. We reserve them for regular prayer meetings, since there is a very definite place for prayers, petitions, and supplications. But in intercession, our priorities take a different shape. First, we cleanse ourselves as the priests did. Then we offer the sweet incense of praise and worship to Him as offerings of our love. That leads to the very heart of prophetic intercession as we wait to find out what is on the Father's heart so we can *speak out* those things and see them come to pass in the earth. This is why we call it *prophetic intercession*. How can anyone know what is on God's heart unless it is imparted by the Spirit?

The Scriptures say that if we pray according to God's will, He will hear and answer. Honestly, I felt "dumber than dirt" when this "new revelation" finally made its way into my brain. How could we have missed something so basic and obvious? (I don't know the answer to that one, but at least I know I had a lot of company in my ignorance.) We've made intercession too difficult when Jesus wants us to tap into the simple pattern He follows as the great Intercessor: He finds out what is on the Father's heart and He prays it. His accuracy record is obviously 100 percent! So what is the secret to this kind of intercessory prayer? Intimacy with God.

Endnotes

1.   Quoted from a transcript of Dale Van Steenis' ministry at Brownsville Assembly of God Church in Pensacola, Florida.

2.   Bobbie Jean Merck, "Fanner Bees & Porters," *A Great Love Overflow* magazine, Vol. 15, No. 2 (Third Quarter, 1992), 3.

3.   *Faith Marches On*, Manifest Deliverance and Worldwide Evangelism, Inc. (May-June, 1961), 24, with the following citation: "This parable was borrowed from an English Journal, author unknown."

4.   Graham Law, "Law's Frequently Asked Questions About Honey Bees," Section 3.8. This United Kingdom entymology expert's material is posted on the University of North Carolina-Chapel Hill Internet site (http://sunsite. unc.edu/pub/academic/agriculture/entomology/beekeeping/faqs/Honey_Bee_Faq193.html).

5.   Law, "Law's Frequently Asked Questions," Sections 3.12–3.14.

6.   Doug Colter, Chief Provincial Inspector, Alberta, Canada; from the article, "Honeybee Activities and Behaviour," reproduced from *Bee News*, Alberta Beekeepers Association Internet site (http://www.albertabeekeepers.org/beenews).

7. Law, "Law's Frequently Asked Questions," Section 2.1–2.2.

8. Law, "Law's Frequently Asked Questions," Section 1.5.

Chapter 3

Ordained for Intimacy

I was an adult before I had heard the gospel of Christ and I knew virtually nothing about God. Therefore, it was only natural for me to live an undesirable adult life until the day I heard that there was Someone who could help me change my life. I didn't hesitate for a moment. I didn't know who Jesus Christ was and I didn't know how to pray, but the night I first heard the gospel and went to the altar in a Brethren in Christ church, I left that altar and never smoked another cigarette, took another drink, or stepped back into my previously unholy lifestyle again.

From that moment on, I had a voracious appetite for God's Word. The only way to describe it was that I was *hungry* for God. It was as if I had waited all my life for the chance to become personally acquainted with God and to love Him with my whole heart. I will never forget the first time I read in the Gospel of Matthew that Jesus said, "Blessed are those who hunger and thirst for righteousness, for they shall be filled" (Mt. 5:6). That was *me*. I was so hungry and thirsty for God and His righteousness that I would consume anything that smelled or hinted of Jesus Christ and my heavenly Father.

A few months after I became a Christian, I was involved in a study of First Corinthians 12 where Paul talks about each of us being a part of the Body in Christ. Someone made the mistake of asking me what part of the Body of Christ I wanted to be, so I said without hesitation, "I want to be a part of the *reproductive system*." Let me explain something quickly so both of us can relax: The "reproductive system" of the Body of Christ is in *the heart* of each believer. God plants His vision and desire in our hearts by His Spirit and helps us bring it to pass on earth as it is in Heaven. There is nothing "sexual" or fleshly here—it is purely by the Spirit.[1] That is why God's Word talks constantly about "the circumcision of the heart." I speak of the spirit, not of the flesh here.

The moment we come to Jesus Christ and receive Him as Lord and Savior, we enter into an eternal covenant with God Himself. We no longer have to make or keep the Old Testament covenants, which required the cutting of flesh to be validated; Jesus paid the supreme price on our behalf already. Yet there is a *circumcision* involved.

Paul tells us, "In Him [Jesus Christ] you were also circumcised with the circumcision made without hands, by putting off the body of the sins of the flesh, by the circumcision of Christ" (Col. 2:11). If you examine the Book of Genesis, you will notice that Abraham was unable to sire the promised seed until after he had been circumcised! This is a type and a shadow of what God is speaking to the Church in this generation. We have a wonderful promise to seize and occupy, but first we must allow Him to cut away the hardness in our hearts by His Spirit and through His Word. We must have hearts of flesh, not hearts of stone.

You will find that the deeper you go into intercession, the more you will be drawn into worship. Reese Howell's description of the three stages of intercession can be found in the book, *Reese Howell, Intercessor* by Norman Percy Grubb. Howell called these stages *identification, agony*, and *authority*.[2] This is a wonderful rule of thumb for intercession, but I would like to add another stage right at the front of the process: *intimacy*. So the expanded progressive stages of prophetic intercession would now be:

1. *Intimacy* with God. Seeking His face rather than His hand.

2. *Identification*. We must identify with His heart and/or those individuals, situations, or purposes He puts on our hearts.

3. *Agony*. In intercession we experience the agony of the crises, problems, or needs of others as if they were our own.

4. *Authority*. We must stand up and declare the heart of God with divine authority borne out of intimacy and identification with Him. (God invests His authority in us because of our obedience.)

The Body of Christ will never be able to move into intercession on the level that God intends for us unless each of us members are drawn into intimacy with the Lord *in our own personal lives*. We have tried to recognize this progression from individual to corporate intimacy in our intercessory prayer meetings. The first thing we do is instruct everyone to cleanse him or herself through Spirit-led examination and repentance of all sin through the shed blood of Jesus Christ. We want to make sure that we enter the Lord's Presence with "clean hands, feet, and hearts." Under the old Aaronic priestly code of the Old Testament, the priests always cleansed themselves before they went in to minister to the Lord. In their case, it was a life and death matter. We take it seriously too, but mostly because our whole focus in prophetic intercession is to *minister to the Lord.*

After we have been cleansed through repentance, we lift holy hands and hearts in praise and worship to God. Sometimes we dance. Sometimes we weep. The truth is that we never really know what we are going to do other than that our goal is to know *what is on God's heart* for us to pray about that evening. He has led us all over the world. We quickly learned that God never intended for His Presence in renewal and revival to be encapsulated in Brownsville Assembly of God or in any other single church or area. Spirit-led and Spirit-directed intercession goes directly into the heavenlies where God releases it anywhere He chooses.

You can go around the world without ever leaving your house or prayer room! Your body may never leave the room, but the Spirit of God may take you into other countries where you will begin to feel the pain of the people there so He can draw you into the agony of their crisis! No, this isn't a Christianette version of a New Age doctrine of astral projection. It is a Pauline experience in the mold of the Macedonian vision in Acts 16:9-15, which birthed the apostle's great work among the Philippians! Out of the agony of that Spirit-birthed intercession will come divine authority to exert God's power over the ruling spirits of darkness in those places.

Dig Out the Riverbed

Soon after we had established the nightly intercessory team, we sensed that God wanted us to allow the revival to expand beyond the four walls of our sanctuary in Pensacola, Florida. He began dealing with the intercessors that it was time to begin building and expanding in the spirit realm. I'll never forget the night He told us, "Dig out the riverbed, widen it, build the banks in praise so that it will begin to flow out to all the different tributaries." The obvious question we asked ourselves and the Lord was, "How do you dig out a river?" In the end, we actually started acting like we were digging out the river (prophetic intercession and prophetic parables again). I realized this was just another step in the fulfillment of God's word to me about trusting Him like children. He promised us if we would do this, then "...He would take us places where we had never been to, we would do things we had never done, hear things we had never heard, and see things that we had never seen." When you live like that, every day is like Christmas! We come into intercession with childlike anticipation because we never know what God is going to do—it is wonderful!

We just began "digging out the bed" of the river with our hands as we worshiped Him. We built up the banks in praise and began to experience a new freedom in our praise and worship. We began to "see" the river of God's Presence widen by the Spirit. Then we saw God's Spirit begin to trickle into other areas and launch revival in other places around North America and the world.

One night in intercession we asked God for the nations, and He shocked us by saying, "I've given you the nations. Now *take* them." This happened just before visitors started to stream in from other nations, and we said, "Lord, we don't know how to take the nations." My personal philosophy and style of intercession is, "If in doubt, dance, worship, and praise God!" So I found a map of the world and put it on the floor. Then we began to literally dance over the nations. Our greatest weapons of spiritual warfare are the high praises of God in our mouths and the two-edged sword of the Spirit (God's Word) in our hands. The enemy has attempted with all his might to keep God's people for discovering the power we have in worship and praise to God, but once again, he has failed.

A Caution From the Lord

The supernatural nature of prophetic intercession and worship and praise in this day sometimes encourages people to go too far. A pastor's wife came to me one night and told me something that almost broke my heart. It drove me to my knees in tears and led me back to the cross. She told me that she and her husband were having some problems with their intercessory prayer group, and I knew my old tape series on intercession covered the particular problem she had mentioned. So I asked, "Has your intercessory prayer group heard my set of audiocassettes on intercession?"[3] She said, "Yes, you are practically 'the god of intercession.' "

With those words, I felt like a sword had been thrust through my heart (not by this dear pastor's wife, but by the Spirit of God). I said, "Oh God, don't ever let that happen. I never want anybody to think that I am some authority or that I am the 'last word.' I'm only one little tiny voice among people who know so much more than I do." I saw a serious danger that needed to be dealt with. When something catches on because God has moved upon it—whether it is a message, a place, or the anointing in your life—the enemy will come against it. If he can't keep people away from it, then he will cause them to idolize it and worship it. May God help us. We are idolatrous by nature, and we need the keeping power of God's grace and mercy in our lives every single day.

God fulfilled His eternal purpose in the resurrection of His Son and birthed the Church in a day, but He didn't stop there. He didn't retire, take a vacation, or "leave the motor running" to go do something else. God has been "up to something" these past two millennia! He has been preparing a people within a people since the Day of Pentecost. Even a casual glance at Church history over the past 100 years reveals an astounding series of revivals gradually growing in an intensity and breadth that are about to culminate in something earth-shaking in scope!

I don't have the time or space to cover every special date or turning point in the last 100 years, but let me point out just a few highlights of God's work among us in this century. In case you haven't noticed, *God is up to something*.

My personal belief is that Israel has been closely intertwined with God's purposes for the Church since the day God blessed Abram, changing his name to Abraham, and promising him many descendants because of his faithfulness (see Gen. 17:5ff). God made an eternal covenant with Abraham and He has always had a heart to draw in Abraham's physical descendants as a hen would gather in and cover her chicks (see Mt. 23:37). Just as Jerusalem and the Jews went through a dark period after the crucifixion of Jesus at the hands of both Jew and Gentile executioners, so the Church had to endure a period called the Dark Ages.

At the dawn of the twentieth century, God sovereignly moved to restore the fullness of the Spirit to the Church. In 1901, Agnes Ozman became the first person to be baptized in the Holy Spirit at Charles Parham's Bible school in Topeka, Kansas, a year after students there began to seek God for more of the Acts 2 experience. Their search for more of God began exactly three years after Thodor Herzl founded the Zionist Movement in Basel, Switzerland, to seek the creation "for the Jewish people a home in Palestine secured by public law."[4] This three-year period marked the beginning, the first trickling of a waterfall that would change the face of world history forever for both Israel and the Church. Neither group realized that dark war clouds would also soon descend on the world.

By the time World War I had begun, God had accelerated His restoration movements on both fronts. He ignited a fire in Evan Roberts who, in turn, lit the fires of the Welsh Worldwide Revival in 1905, which had a great influence on all Great Britain and hungry Christians in North America.

The "Pentecostals" in the United States, birthed in the great outpouring of the Holy Spirit in the Azusa Street Revival in Los Angeles, California, had grown enough in numbers and strength to establish such organizations as the Church of God in Christ (1906) and the Assemblies of God (1914). Meanwhile, favor was growing in Great Britain for the establishment of a Jewish homeland in Palestine. In 1917, the British government issued the Balfour Declaration that officially supported the Zionist dream of a Jewish homeland and state. God was obviously serious about restoring the descendants of Abraham to their ancient home in Israel as well.

The world, the Church, and the Jewish community worldwide were rocked by World War II and shocked by the Holocaust, in which Adolf Hitler and his Nazi regime nearly succeeded in ruthlessly exterminating every Jew in Germany and in the nations he dominated or occupied. Millions of unarmed civilian Jews were slaughtered, and hundreds of thousands of Allied and Axis soldiers lost their lives during that seven-year conflict. However, God was not sleeping and He heard the cries of Jews and Christians alike.

In 1947, God released a new wave of salvation and healing meetings through the "Pentecostal" ministries of several bold healing-evangelists, including A.A. Allen, William Branham, Jack Coe, Oral Roberts, T.L. and Daisy Osborne, and Kathryn Kuhlman, just to name a few. And, of course, I should mention a little-known healing evangelist from Lancaster, California, named Tommy Hicks who was known for his baggy trousers, worn-out shoes, and passion for prayer.

That same year, Great Britain announced that it would pull its troops out of Palestine by August of 1948, and asked the United Nations to take over. The U.N. called its first ever "special session" and on November 29, 1947, it voted to partition Palestine into separate Jewish and Arab states— in effect, officially granting a homeland for displaced Jews for the first time in centuries! War broke out on May 15, 1948, when five Arab states joined with Arab guerrilla forces to attack the one-day old state of Israel. The "war of independence" didn't last long, but it resulted in Israel expanding its borders beyond the original U.N. guidelines by nearly 8,000 square miles!

In 1949, three additional events occurred that demonstrated an uncanny parallel between events in the Church and in tiny Israel. A young Youth for Christ evangelist named Billy Graham was conducting evangelistic tent meetings in downtown Los Angeles when a man shot at him with a pistol. This incident spawned unprecedented publicity for the determined young preacher, and his three-week crusade was expanded to eight weeks to accommodate the standing-room only crowds that flocked to the meetings. As of this writing, Dr. Graham has preached the uncompromising gospel of Christ to more than 210 million people in person in more than 185 countries, with hundreds of millions more being reached through the media.[5]

It was also in 1949 that Israel's Provisional State Council organized elections for the first Knesset (parliament), essentially organizing Israel's first official government body since the nation was nearly obliterated and dispersed centuries ago under the oppression of the Roman Empire. Meanwhile, a discouraged missionary named Edward Miller was driven to his knees in prayer in Argentina, far from the events of Washington, Los Angeles, Tel Aviv, and Jerusalem. But his prayers, and those of three timid prayer warriors, were about to help birth a revival that would change the world. The third event marking 1949 as a watershed year of the Spirit was the founding of the Latter Rain movement in Canada, which emphasized the then-radical belief that God was pouring out His Spirit on all flesh in this century, complete with all the prophetic gifts and the signs and wonders seen in the first century Church.

The 1950's saw the great conflict between Communism and the free world crystallize in the tension of a divided Berlin and in the explosive situation in the Korean Conflict when Communist Chinese troops crossed the border to directly engage U.S. troops in battle. Demos Shakarian founded the Full Gospel Businessmen's Fellowship International in 1951 to bring the vibrant message of Christ and the fullness of the Spirit to the formerly closed circles of the business community worldwide. In 1954, Tommy Hicks preached the gospel to record crowds in Argentina where three and a half million people came to Christ in only 62 days (T.L. and Daisy Osborne were already ministering with great anointing in Chile at the time as well), and revival fires began to sweep throughout South America.[6]

Tommy Hicks continued to spread the fire at home and abroad through the early 1960's. The Assemblies of God and C.M. Ward launched *Revivaltime* ministries and David Yonggi Cho planted a church in Seoul, South Korea. Meanwhile, Israel was again attacked by Egypt and ended up capturing and holding the Gaza Strip until early 1957. In 1959, an Episcopal priest named Dennis Bennett announced over the radio that he had "spoken in tongues," and the Charismatic movement began to introduce the Pentecostal experience to thousands of hungry Roman Catholics, Episcopalians, Presbyterians, Methodists, and more.

In 1967, Israel was once more embroiled in war, the infamous "Six-Day War" with Egypt, Jordan, and Syria. This time, Israel totally humiliated her attackers, even though their forces were much larger and better equipped, and she ended up capturing so much land that her borders were *four times larger* than they had been following her 1949 battles! Meanwhile, David Wilkerson had published *The Cross and the Switchblade*, the story of his miraculous ministry to inner-city gangs in New York City; and countless numbers of young ministers began to invade the hippie counterculture in Southern California and across the United States. The Jesus movement was born, sweeping thousands of "hippies" and other young people into the Church and the Pentecostal experience. This "battle" of the Kingdom with the rebellious drug culture of the U.S. permanently changed the face of American Christianity. The "borders" of the Church were permanently expanded to the "streets." It was also in 1967 that the Roman Catholic Charismatic renewal began in Pittsburgh, Pennsylvania.

In 1973, Israel was the victim of a massive secret attack on Yom Kippur (Passover), the holiest of all Jewish fasts and religious holidays. The Jews managed to drive back her attackers, but at a great cost of lives, economic stability, and unity. The excitement of the Jesus movement was beginning to wane, and splinter cults such as "Moses" David Berg's Children of God brought division and public disapproval to the greater—and purer—move of God among the restless youth of America.[7]

The 1980's found Israel struggling to regain her footing economically and politically from the debts created by war and from her need to maintain a large standing army for defense. No single political party was able to effectively lead the nation, and Israel's coffers were being constantly drained by a nagging problem with PLO guerrillas entrenched in Lebanon, the Israeli invasion of Beirut, and the occupation of Southern Lebanon. In the United States, the Charismatic elements of the Church had lost direction and suffered some of its greatest challenges through cultural and spiritual apathy, and the excesses and moral failure of prominent Charismatic televangelists.

In 1994, Israel signed an historic peace agreement with King Hussein of Jordan, which ended 46 years of war and antagonism, and established diplomatic relations with the Vatican. In 1995, Israel and the PLO signed a second peace agreement, and by 1996, the PLO had voted to officially abolish the sections of its charter calling for Israel's destruction.

Meanwhile, God visited a small Vineyard fellowship in Toronto, Ontario, in January of 1994, astounding the Christian world with the intensity of His love. In May, He touched a reserved audience at the respected Holy Trinity Brompton Anglican Church in London with the same anointing, and later fell on the congregation of the Sunderland Christian Centre in Sunderland, England. Then the Lord descended on Florida, bringing renewal to Melbourne, Florida, in 1995 and electrifying a surprised Assembly of God congregation in Pensacola, Florida, by "descending suddenly" on their Sunday meeting on Father's Day of 1995.

As of this writing, Israel is about to celebrate its first "year of Jubilee" since the crucifixion of Christ and the destruction of Jerusalem! And in the same month of April in 1998, Good Friday, Passover, and Easter are all being celebrated on the same weekend, despite the differences between the Julian calendar and the Jewish religious calendar! This cannot be a coincidence, especially when you realize that the Festival of Firstfruits is celebrated one week after Passover, and that Passover also marks the beginning of the Festival of Weeks, a 50-week harvest festival that we call *Pentecost*. Something of global proportions is about to explode on the earth, and I'm glad to be alive to see it! I am convinced that God is about to inaugurate a harvest of monumental proportions! In other words, "You ain't seen nothin' yet!"

These are only the briefest of highlights, because God has been at work *continuously* over the years in places too numerous to count! He sparked revival fires in South America that never went out, even though the believers there experienced alternating periods of revival and "recession." God sparked revival simultaneously on both American coasts, not merely in Florida, in 1994 and 1995, as well as in key places around the world. Let me emphasize again that this magnificent move of God cannot be attributed to the work of any one individual, congregation, group, or geographical location. God has and is using countless local congregations, individuals, and even the secular media to accomplish His purposes in this generation, and He has only just begun![8]

I noticed a historical pattern that is worthy of mention, although I don't propose to make it a doctrine or even a prediction. But God seems to move upon His Church in dramatic ways just before major crises in the earth. He moved on His Church just before the American Revolutionary War, before the American Civil War, before World Wars I and II, before the Korean Conflict, and before and during the Vietnam War. The Lord even used the two-and-a-half-month

Gulf War in 1991 to mobilize prayer on a level rarely seen in America since the Korean Conflict or before.

The single most prominent thread I see in the Lord's movements among the nations in this century is a call to *intimacy with God*. People of every culture seem to be longing for "something more" than the status quo. He seems to be planting a longing in human hearts that can no longer be satisfied by religion as usual or by carefully doled out, fire-proofed, and processed glimpses of a supernatural God through "politically correct" theology. He starts by planting hunger in us, and then He shows up in unexpected ways and places at unexpected times—just to remind us that He is God and we are not.

Whatever happens, I believe we are seeing more than a temporary revival sweeping through the world. I believe God is moving to raise up a worldwide army of intercessors to pray for a harvest of unprecedented proportions! If you feel like you've "arrived late to the party," let me give you a word of encouragement. This "soul-winning party" is just beginning. You may feel like I felt the first time I visited the revival services at Brownsville Assembly of God in Pensacola. I was *graced* into this revival. When my husband and I decided to move from Southern California to Mississippi in 1993, we had never been to Brownsville. (Our new home was located less than two hours from Pensacola.) We moved simply because we believed that we were being led of the Lord. We left a church where we had served as associate pastors for ten years and had been working with a pastor whom we loved. We had all worked wonderfully together with no problems, but when God said to move, we moved.

Meanwhile, we visited Toronto to investigate "the blessing" in May of 1995 because we felt so dry and thirsty for more of God. (We were blessed during our visit, but frankly, I was afraid that by moving to a little community in Mississippi that God was going to move and we were going to miss it!) When we finally heard about the revival at Brownsville and visited the church, it was the most wonderful thing I had ever experienced in my life. Even at that point, only three weeks into the revival, we couldn't get into the main auditorium because we arrived only 15 minutes before the service. I sat in the chapel, but I literally didn't want to leave or go home. I didn't even have to be prayed for. It was enough just to sit there in the Presence of the Lord because I was so dry and so thirsty. I felt so grateful that God had shown up someplace and that it was close enough to my home that I could visit. I never dreamed that within three months of that visit Pastor John Kilpatrick would ask me to head the intercessory prayer department at Brownsville Assembly of God.

By the time the Brownsville revival had reached its three-month mark, Pastor Kilpatrick believed that it needed to be "guarded" (not *controlled)* and uplifted in prayer. Intercessory prayer and regular prayer meetings had been conducted faithfully for years, but Pastor Kilpatrick felt that the Lord was asking for something unique, something more than was in place at the time. He believed God wanted the church to maintain intercession on a nightly basis to guard the purity of what God was doing from the pollution of the flesh and religious tradition. That was when I was invited to come and to head the intercession. I told the leadership there that I would have to pray about it, and I did.

I prayed, "Lord, I haven't been here with these people for the two-and-a-half years of weekly prayer meetings they have sacrificed in the building of the church, all the personal sacrifices the people have made, nor all their time of preparation. How is it going to look to the Brownsville people when someone from the 'outside' comes in to head something as important as the intercessory prayer department?" He answered, "You haven't sown at Brownsville, but you *have sown*. You have been sowing into My Kingdom all these years. You haven't been sowing into yourself, or your own ministry, or your husband's ministry. You have been sowing into the Kingdom of God, and that is where the harvest is coming from."

When God said these things to me, I was off my knees and dialing the phone number for Brownsville Assembly of God as fast as I could! I said, "Yes, I'll be right there." So know this, even if you come up dry where you have been fishing, God will give you a harvest even if He has to lead you to another hole!

I spoke not too long ago with Dr. Ed Miller, and he said that during the second great revival in Argentina from 1968 until 1973, most of the services were devoted to *worship*. Many souls were saved, but in unusual ways. People would come in and the power of God would be so intense in those meetings that the holiness of God would reveal the reality of their sinful nature and they would fall on their faces crying out for mercy—even without a sermon or an altar call. Sometimes people couldn't even come through the door because of the Presence of the Lord. I call this "salvation by His Presence." He did it once, and I have news for you: He's doing it again at Brownsville and countless other places around the world!

The other thing Dr. Miller mentioned to me and referenced throughout his book, *Cry for Me Argentina*, is the fact that God tends to manifest or reveal His glory with unusual power in those places where a price has been paid in the past, or where He has previously poured out His Spirit. We often see His glory visiting new generations in places where His image still lingers from a previous visitation....

Endnotes

1. It is important for you to understand this distinction. There are a lot of strange and extra-biblical doctrines floating around out there in "intercessor land" that are in absolute error! One of these is the "bridal chamber experience." Cindy Jacobs encountered this phenomenon and was told by the Lord that she was dealing with an "incubus spirit," an unclean spirit sent to prey on women in particular, using sexual advances, illusions, and temptations. My counsel to anyone who believes that he or she is being somehow "sexually aroused" in any way during prayer comes directly from First John 4:1a, "Beloved, do not believe every spirit, but test the spirits, whether they are of God." For more information on this dangerous area of error, see *Posessing the Gates of the Enemy* by Cindy Jacobs (Grand Rapids, Michigan: Baker Books, 1994).

2. Norman Percy Grubb, *Reese Howell, Intercessor* (London: Lutterworth Press, 1952), 81.

3. I have a 15-part audiotape series with a workbook that some churches have used to train their intercessory prayer people. It presents the basics of intercession as a

foundation, while the contents of this book go far beyond that foundational level. Of course, no book (other than God's Word) can present itself as the ultimate source of information or understanding. We will all continue to learn, grow, and expand as we move deeper into His Presence.

4. "Israel," *Microsoft Encarta 97 Encyclopedia* (Microsoft Corporation, 1993–1996).

5. Excerpted from the biography of Billy Graham provided by the Billy Graham Evangelistic Association at its Internet site: http://www.graham-assn.org/bgea. Updated 8/97.

6. These incredible figures were printed in numerous publications by Evangelist Tommy Hicks. This specific reference was found in two issues of *Faith Marches On* Vol. 2, No. 1 (Los Angeles: Manifest Deliverance and Worldwide Evangelism, Inc., 1960), on the back cover with a picture of Argentines gathered in the Atlanta Stadium during an altar call in Buenos Aires; and in Vol. 2, No. 4 (April, 1960), 4.

7. For more information, you might want to see "History of the Jesus Movement," a research thesis written by Dave DiSabatino after he conducted two years of study and personal interviews. Contact Mr. DiSabatino directly by e-mail at sabbi@the-wire.com or at the following address: 2008 Aldermead Rd., Mississauga, Ontario, L5M 3A7, Canada. As of this writing, it is available for review on the Internet at http://www.ldolphin.org/jpindex.shtml. The author also provides an excellent list of sources for further research.

8. If you would like more details about the incredible breadth and depth of this current move of God, I

recommend "A History of the Worldwide Awakening of 1992–1995," 11th edition, written and published by Richard M. Riss, through the Toronto Airport Christian Fellowship Internet site: http://www.tacf.org. Mr. Riss is a Church historian who, as of this writing, teaches Church history at Zarephath Bible Institute, New Jersey, an affiliate of Asbury Theological Seminary, Wilmore, Kentucky. He is a Ph.D. candidate with Drew University, Madison, New Jersey, and is the author of several books, including *Images of Revival* published by Destiny Image Publishers.

Chapter 4

Where His Image Still Lingers

"On September 7, 1850, Captain Allen Gardiner sailed for Patagonia, the southern portion of Argentina, with six other men...Gardiner's burden was: 'Our Savior has given a commandment to preach the Gospel even to the ends of the earth. He will provide the fulfillment of His own purpose. Let us only obey.' Knowing that Patagonia, the extreme south land of Argentina, is a barren desert-like land, the men took, what they thought to be, ample supplies...

"...After much fatigue and privation from want of food and while waiting on the sea shore for the supply ship to come, Allen Gardiner and his men departed into the presence of their Lord between June 8 and September 8, 1851. The ship laden with the needed supplies of food did not reach the seven men until several months too late...

"...Ragland, a pioneer missionary to India, wrote, 'Of all plans of insuring success, the most certain is Christ's own—becoming a corn of wheat, falling into the ground and dying. Verily, verily, I say unto you, Except a corn of wheat fall into the ground and die, it abideth alone; but if it die, it bringeth forth much fruit.' "

Stanley Frodsham[1]

When archaeologists unearthed the ancient tombs of the Pharaohs, they found honeycomb that had been stored as "food" for the deceased kings in the afterworld. The honey they found inside was as fresh and sweet as the day it had been stored by bees in Egypt 3,000 years before. It was virtually untouched by the passage of time![2] In a much greater way, prayer is not restricted to the limitations of time or space as we are. Intercession that is birthed in the Spirit of God literally crosses the ages and transcends our years to bear fruit in fields we know nothing about.

In a sense, our prayers are like eternal honey, the condensed nectar of God, a sweet delight to His tongue and fragrance in His nostrils. He never "misplaces" or ignores the fervent prayers of the righteous. The Scriptures tell us that He likens our prayers to holy incense, and carefully stores them like treasure to be poured out, enjoyed, and speedily answered in His divine timing (see Rev. 5:8; 8:3-4). The truth of the matter is that many of us would not be here today if it were not for the fervent prayers of grandparents, parents, and other intercessors who have lived and gone into the heavenly realm before us—leaving an eternal memorial of prayer behind as a life-giving store of heavenly honey or holy incense.

We know the prophets and patriarchs of ancient Israel saw by the Spirit into the heavenlies, looking by faith "for a heavenly city" and the coming of the Messiah.

These all died in faith, not having received the promises, but having seen them afar off were assured of them, embraced them and confessed that they were strangers and pilgrims on the earth. For those who say such things declare plainly that they seek a homeland. And truly if they had called to mind that country from which they had come out, they would have had opportunity to return. But now they desire a better, that is, a heavenly country. Therefore God is not ashamed to be called their God, for He has prepared a city for them (Hebrews 11:13-16).

God never forgets our labors of love in prayer. A great hunger for revival is sweeping across ancient Scotland where John Knox poured out his life and prayers for his kinsmen hundreds of years ago. Although he is with the Lord today, his voice is still speaking from the grave every time his fervent prayers are poured out of golden censers before the throne, filling the nostrils of God with remembrance.

Dr. Edward Miller adds a sequel to the brief excerpt you read about the sacrifice of faith and mission made by Captain Gardiner and his companions in 1850 that is astounding. It concerns what happened after the young wife who came to Dr. Miller's prayer vigil along with her backslidden husband and a timid servant girl finally "struck the table" in obedience to God. He writes:

"It was in early June, 1949, that the River from heaven began to flow out into the city of Mendoza, in Argentina. Precisely, it was the same city and the only city in Argentina that one hundred years earlier had accepted and listened to Allen Gardiner and his band who had laid down their lives for Argentina. That city, Mendoza, a century later was the place the seed, planted so long before, began to sprout and flourish."[3]

Many other missionaries and believers have laid down their lives for Christ because of their love and mission to the nations. God has those prayers sitting as a memorial before Him. Many He answered long ago, some only recently, and a few remain to be answered. God never forgets.

I'm very aware of our indebtedness—to the Lord Jesus Christ first and foremost, but also to all those who have gone before us in faith, obedience, and sacrifice. As you read this book, my prayer is that you will see Christ emerge from the page rather than some inflated view of my excellence or skill in prayer. I come humbly before you with "shared bread" from His Presence, not as some expert on intercession. (Honestly, I may well know less about it than you do!) So if you picked up this book and gathered together your pens, pencils, and paper to take notes as you learn "how to have revival," then I have a confession to make: not one person in Brownsville knows how!

Yes, we prayed corporately for 30 months or so, but we also know of individuals and church congregations that have prayed faithfully for 8, 10, or even 25 years who are still waiting for revival to come. God has His own purpose and reasons. We are simply grateful that He opened the heavens over Brownsville and has brought in the nations. The leadership at Brownsville Assembly of God is painfully aware that there are no guarantees that God will "show up" in His glory tomorrow or next week. He alone knows. We just thank Him for His visitation of glory today and for yesterday, and we will look eagerly for His Presence tomorrow.

One of the most persistent words that God uses in His Word appears in the very first chapter of the Bible, and it appears again and again in the New Testament as well. It is the word *image*. There are two very well-known applications to "image," which I will cover briefly here, although you are probably well acquainted with them. Yet there is a third application that you may know little or nothing about that is of growing importance in God's move across the earth today.

Created in His Image

*Then God said, "Let Us make man in **Our image**, according to **Our likeness**; let them have dominion over the fish of the sea, over the birds of the air, and over the cattle, over all the earth and over every creeping thing, that creeps on the earth." So God created man in His own image; in the image of God He created him; male and female He created them* (Genesis 1:26-27).

You and I and every other human being on this planet were created in God's image. He breathed His life-giving Spirit into us, animating our soul (the seat of our reason and emotions), and bringing life to our physical body. The image we were born with is a faint echo of what God intends because Adam and Eve fell through sin. We are missing the crown of our three-part being, the breath of His eternal Spirit, until the day we repent of our sins and receive Jesus Christ as Lord and Savior. (I won't get into the state of unsaved infants in any detail, but I believe they are covered in God's grace until they are old enough to make a true decision and commitment to Christ with all their being.)

God is out to restore the intimate fellowship that He shared daily with Adam and Eve as they walked in the cool of the garden together. (Remember that God did not draw back from mankind; we drew back from God.) Jesus Christ, God's Son, entered our world through the human bloodline of Abraham. Then He perfectly kept the Law of Moses and lived a life without sin until the day He voluntarily laid His life down on the cross and took upon Himself all our sin. In that moment, the possibility of the "garden strolls" became a reality for us. Now it is up to us, but it will cost us something. First, we were created in God's image, and promptly lost it. Through Jesus, we regain His breath (the first part of the Genesis story—He created us in His image and breathed life into us). Now He wants to shape us into His *likeness* (see Gen. 1:26a).

Conformed to His Image

*For whom He foreknew, He also predestined **to be conformed to the image of His Son**, that He might be the firstborn among many brethren. Moreover whom He predestined, these He also called; whom He called, these He also justified; and whom He justified, **these He also glorified*** (Romans 8:29-30).

When Christ came into your spirit, you were "DNA'd" with His image. In the natural or physical realm, DNA is the genetic code, or "blueprint," for the cells that make up all living things. The core DNA strand for you will be the same whether researchers examine cells from your hair samples, toenail clippings, or from a liver biopsy. In a very real sense, God has implanted within your physical DNA the sum total of your physical potential in your lifetime. It is the same in the spirit. When you were born again, the Holy Spirit DNA'd you with the image of Christ. The problem is that most of us have embraced a false image of God and of ourselves as Christians, which is just another definition for idolatry.

We tend to spell *God* with a little "g." (We'd never admit it, of course.) We have actually "demoted" God in our minds by trying to bring Him down to "our level" in our thinking and in our actions. However, He will have none of it. He wants to bring us up to *His level*, and to conform us to *His image*. That is why He is surprising His Church so often in our generation. He is quickly shattering all the limiting, misinformed images we have of Him, the images that say, "Well, God would *never* do that. He is too dignified to make people do that. He can move this way, but never that way." Thousands of Christians and non-Christians around the world are discovering that God really is God, and He can do anything He pleases—with or without our permission!

Revisiting God's Image in the "Ancient Wells"

In August of 1997, Marc Dupont said something remarkable in an interview with *Destiny Image Digest* Managing Editor Larry Walker that has everything to do with this third understanding of God's image on the earth. Marc Dupont is a prophet, a man recognized for his conservative but accurate prophetic insights into the workings of God. He spoke of "ancient wells" from previous anointings or visitations of God, where He made "deposits of glory":

"We're about to see a tremendous move of God that will be transdenominational. God wants to *dig up the ancient wells* where there are *deposits of glory*, whether it's a past Mennonite movement or a Quaker movement or a Baptist, Lutheran, or Anglican thing. But it won't be by denomination; it will be church by church. It'll be whether we respond or not. In other words, there'll be one Baptist church experiencing a fullness of God's Spirit and where lives are changing, and another Baptist church where it's not happening. There'll be one Vineyard church where it's happening, and another where it's not. And people in the community will say, '*God's in* **this** *church, but He's* **not** *in that church.*' "[4]

I've come to understand that what Marc Dupont calls "ancient wells" are places where God's image lingers on from previous visitations and impartations of His glory. The great Argentine revival exploded in 1954 when Tommy Hicks came to Buenos Aires. However, the *first-fruits* of that harvest came to Mendoza, Argentina, in 1949 when Dr. Edward Miller came there immediately after the consecrated prayer and angelic visitations at the Bible Institute in City Bell. Mendoza was the only city to respond with open hearts 100 years earlier when Captain Allen Gardiner and his companions dug the first well of the gospel in Argentina with their own lives. It was no accident that the fire of revival first blazed in Mendoza. God's image and glory had never left the place. Mendoza was a tinderbox of the Holy Ghost containing a storehouse of combustible glory just waiting for the match of faith and anointing to spark true revival!

The Argentine revival also vividly demonstrated the reality of "territorial spirits" to modern evangelicals. After revival broke out in 1954, Christian workers had no trouble preaching the gospel wherever they went in Argentina. All they had to say was, "gospel meeting," and large crowds sometimes numbering into the thousands would gather. This was exactly opposite to the situation missionaries and Argentine believers faced before that time. Dr. Miller remembers an experiment done to verify the prophetic word that the "strongman" over Argentina had been bound.

Some gospel workers went to a street shared by Argentina on one side and Bolivia on the other. When the workers handed out tracts on the Bolivian side, they met great opposition. One woman in particular refused to even accept a gospel tract. Yet once the *same woman* crossed over to the Argentine side of the street, the workers approached her again and she warmly received the tract! This pattern continued all that day. Everyone gladly received the tracts on the Argentine side of the street and everyone refused them on the Bolivian side. This principle has been studied and strategies of spiritual warfare have been developed accordingly in recent decades. This has been documented by Dr. C. Peter Wagner of Fuller Theological Seminary in conjunction with Evangelist Carlos Annacondia and Ed Silvoso, director of Harvest Evangelism in San Jose, California, and author of *That None Should Perish.*[5] The plan, called "spiritual mapping," involves researching the spiritual and natural history of a city or region for evidence of demonic strongholds in the area. This in turn helps guide intercessory prayer efforts in that area. I agree that this is very useful and effective when it is part of God's ordained methodology. Much of

Argentina has been systematically "mapped" and released from spiritual bondage through this type of ministry.

Encountering His Lingering Image

However, I've been struck by the positive side of spiritual mapping as well. God has been speaking earnestly to me about His lingering image in our cities, towns, and regions. This was driven home to me during a trip to Sunderland, England, during two supernatural encounters with God. My hosts were Ken and Lois Gott, the founders of Revival Now!, who pastored the former Sunderland Christian Centre where the glory of God fell much as it has in Brownsville. They took me to the site of a small Anglican church in Sunderland where there was a small outpouring of the Holy Ghost in the previous century. A plumber named Smith Wigglesworth came to Sunderland from London, hoping to experience this "baptism in the Holy Spirit" that he had heard about.

After several disappointing days at the meetings, Wigglesworth reluctantly decided to make his way back home. But he decided to try one last time and knocked on the door of Alexander Boddy, the evangelical Anglican vicar of All Saints Parish Church, who was leading the revival. The vicar wasn't home, but Mrs. Boddy agreed to pray for him right there in her kitchen. And it was right there in Mrs. Boddy's kitchen that the great Smith Wigglesworth was baptized in the Holy Ghost and fire "at the hands of a woman" on October 28, 1907. He didn't receive it until *after* the meetings because God wanted him to receive it at the hands of a woman! You probably know that the world was never the same again because God touched Wigglesworth with fire and glory that day, and he took it everywhere he went until the day he died. When the Gotts and I visited that small church, the glory that came upon Brother Boddy and All Saints Parish Church was still lingering there, though the generation of that day is largely gone. It is no wonder that the three of us couldn't do anything but prophesy in that place; God's image was still lingering there.

A second experience also occurred in Sunderland in the auditorium of the main Revival Now! church congregation. The Gotts and I had no sooner stepped onto the platform than we just sort of fell over! I kept saying, "What in the world is this? Why is the power of God so mighty here?" The Gotts told me, "Well, actually, this building was built over the very courtyard where John Wesley used to preach the gospel." I said, "No wonder." Later on, I asked why Wesley had been preaching to people in a courtyard *outside* of the church building that used to stand on that spot, and I was told that the local church leaders wouldn't let him in the church to preach. (Some things never change.)

Many people have taken the dynamic truths of spiritual warfare and spiritual mapping far beyond the proper bounds. These tools are incredibly useful when God tells us to use them, but they can be destructive too if they are used outside of God's direction. In general, we need to be more concerned about *what God is revisiting*. My concern is for those intercessors who tend to get their eyes fixed on "where the devil is working" and are being overcome with the power of darkness. When God moves in an area and the Holy Spirit shows up in power and glory, the enemy will try to follow behind to superimpose himself and his minions in that area for the next generation. As a result, all they ever see is the devil in that place. (That was the case in Mendoza. Dr. Miller reports that it was very difficult to break through in that town at first—it took the sovereign power of God in signs and wonders of healing to break the enemy's deception in that town.)

In those places where God has already established something long ago, all we need to do is go in boldly and begin to worship and praise the name of Jesus. As we lift Him up, His glory will dispel and lift the powers of darkness off of that place and release the glory of His image or Presence again.

Discover where and when God has moved in your area. Get the prophecies given over your city and region. Interview the older saints who have been around a long time. Ask them if there has ever been a major move of God in your area. Begin to talk to other intercessors who may have already done this kind of research. Then you can begin to pray these historical things back to God in reverent remembrance. Discover God's mind and will for your area and church and then begin to pray accurate and focused prayers for focused results! There are a billion things that you could pray about, but it is best to pray what is on the heart of God. He is pouring out His Spirit around the world today, and that should confirm to you that He wants revival more than we do!

Changed in His Presence

I believe that every time we come into the Presence of the Lord, we are changed. Whether it is in a corporate meeting or in our private times of prayer or devotions, we will be changed. This is what Paul meant when he said, "But we all, with unveiled face, beholding as in a mirror the glory of the Lord, *are being transformed into the same image from glory to glory*, just as by the Spirit of the Lord" (2 Cor. 3:18). Some people are being changed quicker than others because they spend more time in the Presence of the Lord! The principle is simple: The more time you spend with the Lord, the more you will look like Him.

God doesn't do this merely for our own enjoyment—He does it to spread His *glory* over the whole earth one person at a time. If I have been changed into His image, then it stands to reason that I will carry that glory with me just as Moses' face shone with the reflection of God's glory in Exodus 34:29-30. God wants me to display His unveiled glory when I go about my daily chores and do my shopping at the grocery store and the mall. C.S. Lewis hinted at this in his book, *The Great Divorce*, in a passage of dialogue concerning an "average" woman on earth who was considered a "great one" in Heaven:

> "...the abundance of life she [the saint] has in Christ from the Father flows over into them [the people and even the animals around her]...It is like when you throw a stone into a pool, and the concentric waves spread out further and further. Who knows where it will end? Redeemed humanity is still young, it has hardly come to its full strength. But already there is joy enough in the little finger of a great saint such as yonder lady to waken all the dead things of the universe into life."[6]

This is just an inkling of what God intends to do with His image displayed through His people! But God has to do it, because revival and glory come from God alone, not from people or the works they do. We can go through all the mechanics and do all the things that we think we should do to spark revival, but the bottom line is that apart from the work of the Holy Spirit and the Presence of God, we will not have revival.

Paul wrote, "And as we have borne the image of the man of dust, we shall also bear the image of the heavenly Man" (1 Cor. 15:49). I realize that the context of this passage is the resurrection, but I believe that God wants us—as the Church—to bear His image in this earth in ways we have never seen before.

God Is Revisiting the Ancient Places

Get ready, Azusa Street and Los Angeles. God is going to move on the West Coast. He is going to retrace His steps and pour out His glory anew where He has moved in the past, and for a very important reason—His image is still lingering there.

In John 20:25b, Thomas the disciple told his fellow disciples, "Unless I see in His hands the print of the nails, and put my finger into the print of the nails, and put my finger into His side, I will not believe." The Psalmist declared, "The earth is the Lord's, and all its fullness, the world and those who dwell therein" (Ps. 24:1). In the Book of Revelation we read, "All who dwell on the earth will worship Him, whose names have not been written in the Book of Life of the Lamb slain from the foundation of the world" (Rev. 13:8). The apostle Peter assured us that before the foundation of the world everything was done in Christ Jesus (see 1 Pet. 1:19-20). So when Jesus Christ formed this earth, the nail prints were already in His hands so that His image of His redemption was stamped all over this earth! Let that thought sink in.

All the earth and all creation belongs to Him, and He is just waiting for the Church to take it back. It already bears His image and the marks of His redeeming suffering from one end of the earth to the other. Creation bears the "Maker's mark" of the holy Lamb of God, slain before the foundation of the world. Have you ever wondered why the Book of Revelation speaks of "the Lamb slain from the foundation of the world"? (See Revelation 13:8, quoted in the previous paragraph.) That means that in the heavenlies, Jesus had the nail scars in His hand before the world was ever formed.

The image of Christ can be found in another place in the earth too—wherever blood has been shed for righteousness' sake. Genesis 4:10 tells us that Abel's blood still *speaks* or cries out to God from the ground. (Isn't it sad that the very first murder in the earth was rooted in anger over "doctrine"?) This is echoed in the Book of Revelation:

When He opened the fifth seal, I saw under the altar the souls of those who had been slain for the word of God and for the testimony which they held. And they cried with a loud voice, saying, "How long, O Lord, holy and true, until You judge and avenge our blood on those who dwell on the earth?" Then a white robe was given to each of them; and it was said to them that they should rest a little while longer, until both the number of their fellow servants and their brethren, who would be killed as they were, was completed (Revelation 6:9-11).

The voice of every martyr, slain missionary, and innocent still cries out to God from underneath His holy altar in
Heaven, and the Lord hears each one. Not one drop of blood
or cry of the heart is wasted or squandered. It has been said
that the blood of missionaries and martyrs are the seeds of the
harvest, and the "vengeance" they cry out for has nothing to
do with violence toward their persecutors or killers—it is for
the fulfillment of their mission of love. They gave their lives
to see people come to Christ. Yes, the blood still speaks from
under the altar, but it is crying out for the harvest!

If nothing else in this book ever sticks in your memory
or your spirit, make sure this statement does: *No prayer that
you've ever prayed by the Spirit of God will go unanswered!*
It is absolutely impossible for such prayers to be disregard-
ed, because they are the embodiment of the very heart of
God. They are eternal memorials before the throne of God!

Don't be discouraged. If you have prayed for revival and
poured out your heart in prayer for souls, take courage. You
didn't "miss God." Those prayers will follow you, and in
God's time they will come to pass. During the previously
mentioned ministry trip to Moldova with Brenda Kilpatrick
and "Hear O Israel" Ministries, something happened that
illustrated the reality of most of the things mentioned in this
chapter on God's image. Moldova is situated between
Romania and the Ukraine, and we were scheduled to conduct an outreach meeting for the Jewish community in the
capital city of Kishinev. Before I went, I tried unsuccessful-
ly to learn about the history of Moldova. In the end, I finally figured out that the Lord probably didn't want me to
know until I got there.

The night before we left for Moldova, a Messianic Jewish prophet prayed for me and said, "Oh, I see an *ancient footprint*, but I don't understand it." I said "I do!" I knew this was God's way of confirming to me that He was about to revisit a place where He'd moved once before. So I went to Kishinev with a real excitement. We discovered that the first Messianic congregation in Moldova had been established right there in Kishinev at the turn of the century. When World War II occurred, nearly the entire Jewish village was annihilated during the Holocaust. Now God was revisiting that city, and He had not forgotten or ignored the cries of His people. Some 5,000 Jews were saved during those outdoor meetings, and some of the new believers were survivors of the Holocaust! God had already placed His footprint in that area and we simply placed our feet into His footprints and reaped a mighty harvest.

God wants to use you in the same way today. My prayer is that He will become the lingering fragrance of our lives. May we leave His life-giving image on everything that we touch!

Endnotes

1. Stanley Frodsham wrote these words in his Foreword to Dr. R. Edward Miller's *Cry for Me Argentina*. He was one of the first ministers of the Pentecostal faith in England and became the editor of the *Pentecostal Evangel*, the official organ of the Assemblies of God of the U.S.A. for 34 years. He is the author of several books chronicling the wonderful works of God in the early years of the twentieth century, including *Smith Wigglesworth: Apostle of Faith*.

2. Graham Law, "Law's Frequently Asked Questions About Honey Bees," Section 2.6, posted on the University of North Carolina-Chapel Hill Internet site (http://sunsite.unc.edu/pub/academic/agriculture/entomology/bee-keeping/faqs/Honey_Bee_Faq193.html).

3. R. Edward Miller, *Thy God Reigneth* (Fairburn, Georgia: Peniel Publications, 1977), Chapter 5, from http://www.peniel-argentina.org.

4. Larry H. Walker, "A Prophet Among Us," *Destiny Image Digest*, Vol. 5, No. 3 (Fall, 1997), 20. Used by permission.

5. Ed Silvoso's book, *That None Should Perish*, is published by Regal Books.

6. C.S. Lewis, *The Great Divorce* (New York: MacMillan Publishing Company, 1946, 1974), 106-107.

Chapter 5

Judah Leads the Way

I was conducting a service in Odessa, Texas, one time when the power of God came over Pastor Kenneth L. Redmon's wife, Dene, while she was at the keyboard during a time of worship. She couldn't control her hands, which made it a bit difficult for her to continue playing the keyboard. The shaking became quite violent, and Dene began thinking, *I've got to control this.* The next thing we knew, she began to speak fluently and with great authority in a language that was absolutely foreign to her and to every one else in the meeting—everybody except one. (Dene said later that it was dramatically different from her usual "prayer language" in the Spirit.)

As soon as Dene had delivered the message in the unknown tongue, she rolled off her seat and onto the floor! Then a gentleman came up from the audience and gave the interpretation of the message in tongues delivered through Dene (her husband, Pastor Ken, was "out of it" on the floor at the time). The interpretation declared, in essence, that

God was pleased with the worship, but "...some had tried to come into His Throne Room through worship, but had not come through the blood of Jesus and could not enter." Dene described to me in her own words what happened next:

"At the end of the service, a non-Pentecostal Odessa pastor, originally from Mexico, came to the platform and motioned for me to come down so he could talk to me. I stepped down, and he told me that his wife had badgered him to come to this meeting, but he did not believe 'in all this Charismatic worship.' He was suffering with back pain anyway, and he kept telling his wife he didn't want to go. She was insistent [thank God for pushy wives, huh?] so he came in late. He said that he had told God that he didn't believe this stuff and if it was real, God would have to *show* him.

"He was from the gold-mining area of Mexico where the Indians speak a dialect instead of Spanish. His family still lives there. When I spoke the message [in an unknown tongue] from the keyboard, it was in his native dialect. I asked him, 'What did I say?' He replied, 'You said what that man said that came up after you: "You cannot come into the Throne Room unless you come through the blood." '

"In addition to God's showing him that the tongues were definintely from Him, the man's back was healed during the service—no laying on of hands, just the power of God."[1]

No Praise, No Presence

It was no accident that this miracle happened during praise and worship. For more than a decade, God has relentlessly moved upon the Church to return to praise and worship in new and deeper ways. He has refused to manifest His Presence among us until we release our deathgrip on our cherished Pentecostal tradition of "three songs and a special." Have you noticed that when you see God moving mightily in a church that it is usually in a place were there is a lot of praise and worship? Why? Because God inhabits the praises of His people (see Ps. 22:3 KJV). The New American Standard Bible says God is *"enthroned upon the praises of Israel."* We literally build a throne for the Almighty One through our praise and worship to Him.

Prayer opens the way for God to move, but worship and praise invite Him to reveal Himself among us—we literally "pull out a seat of honor" for Him when we worship Him. I think we have carelessly overlooked the words of Jesus to the Samaritan woman at the well:

> *But the hour is coming, and now is, when the true worshipers will worship the Father in spirit and truth; **for the Father is seeking such to worship Him*** (John 4:23).

Jesus didn't say that the Father was seeking such to preach for Him, to teach for Him, to conduct or attend seminars for Him, or even to "sit in pews" for Him! (So much for most of our priorities, programs, and practices in the local church.) According to my studies of the Bible, there are three things every church is called to do above all other things:

1. To lift up Jesus so that He can draw all men unto Himself (see Jn. 12:32).

2. To be a house of prayer for all nations (see Mt. 21:13).

3. To be a house of worshipers who worship the Father in spirit and truth (see Jn. 4:23).

I foresee that in the future, entire church congregations will stand and worship God for hours enraptured in His Presence and beauty. Given that kind of atmosphere of devotion to God, He will show up in such a tremendous way that there will be no focus upon one particular person. I believe that healings will spontaneously occur simply because of the Presence of Almighty God. (The Bible tells us in Second Corinthians 3:17b, "...where the Spirit of the Lord is, there is liberty.")

I am not trying to undermine other methods of prayer or minimize the importance of prayer itself. We are told to lift up prayer "of all kinds" at all times, so we need to learn as much about them and their proper uses as we can (see Eph. 6:18). God has a plan, and it involves much more than what we are seeing take place around the world right now. You may disagree with me, but I think this is far greater than simply a one-time refreshing or revival that God is bringing to specific places. I believe that God wants to move throughout the entire world in a history-shattering revelation of His glory.

God has a *redemptive purpose* for every church, city, and region in the earth. One of the things that we need to do as intercessors is to find out the vision of our respective pastors and leadership teams. Then we need to line up with that vision and function as we are ordained to function—as a *helps ministry*. This will directly affect the health of the entire local church body. Aaron and Hur are a picture of the helps ministry of intercession in action in Exodus 17:10-12:

*So Joshua did as Moses said to him, and fought with Amalek. And Moses, Aaron, and Hur went up to the top of the hill. And so it was, when Moses held up his hand, that Israel prevailed; and when he let down his hand, Amalek prevailed. But Moses' hands became heavy; so **they took a stone and put it under him**, and he sat on it. And **Aaron and Hur supported his hands, one on one side, and the other on the other side**; and his hands were steady until the going down of the sun.*

Moses is a type of the modern pastor who wields the shepherd's staff, a staff of responsibility and authority. Notice that this passage later talks about *both* of Moses' hands being lifted over the battle. The hand with the staff represented the authority and protection of God over Israel, and I believe the empty hand represented God's hand of blessing and covenant over His people.

When Moses grew tired, Aaron and Hur came in to help. Aaron represents the high priestly call of every believer (and perhaps our role as intercessors specifically). Hur later became a member of the Sanhedrin, the chief ruling and judicial body of Israel. He represents our call to do "the work of the ministry" as members of Christ's Body and the administrative function in the local church, specifically. What did these men do? They lifted and supported their leader's arms and helped him in his weakness. Please notice that *at no time did they try to remove the rod of authority* from Moses' hand and place it in their own! All they did was lift his hands so he could fulfill his calling in God. When Moses grew weary, they moved the Rock of salvation, Christ Jesus, underneath him so he could function in the "rest" of God. It was the assistance of an "administrator and an intercessor" that let Moses fulfill his function without taking his eyes off of the battle. Intercessor, God may well begin to show you things prophetically, but He will *never* use you to supersede or undermine the leadership He has set in place.

Born to Praise

> *And she* [Leah, wife of Jacob] *conceived again and bore a son, and said, "Now I will praise the Lord." Therefore she called his name Judah. Then she stopped bearing* (Genesis 29:35).

Leah was the "unwanted" wife of Jacob, the older sister of Jacob's favorite wife, Rachel. Leah had three sons before Judah was born, and in each case, she hoped that the birth of these sons would please her husband and win his favor. Later on, she had even more sons and again these children were attempts to win her husband's favor. But Judah was different. Leah turned her eyes away from her husband and herself and said, "I will praise the Lord," and she named this special son *Judah*. The Hebrew version of this word, *Jehudah*, means "celebrated" or praise.[2] It is derived from the Hebrew root *yadah*, which means "to throw a stone or an arrow, especially to revere or worship with extended hands; to bemoan by wringing the hands; to praise, shoot, give thanks."[3] We need to see that the most effective way to defeat the enemy is through praise!

Judah, you are he whom your brothers shall praise; your hand shall be on the neck of your enemies; your father's children shall bow down before you. Judah is a lion's whelp; from the prey, my son, you have gone up. He bows down, he lies down as a lion; and as a lion, who shall rouse him? The scepter shall not depart from Judah, nor a lawgiver from between his feet, until Shiloh comes; and to Him shall be the obedience of the people (Genesis 49:8-10).

Jesus Christ is called the lion of the tribe of Judah (see Rev. 5:5). So He is pictured in Genesis 49 as a warring lion full of strength and power, a warrior. So when we talk about Judah, we talk about warriors, kings, and the lion of Judah. Since Judah means praise, we need to ask God to open our eyes to the eternal value of worship.

Jesus came to fulfill all the Law and the prophets, and God's ultimate plan was to bring the Holy Spirit so that He could communicate with us directly spirit to spirit. So each of us have been made a mobile "holy of holies." That is what is meant by the verse, "Or do you not know that your body is the temple of the Holy Spirit who is in you, whom you have from God, and you are not your own?" (1 Cor. 6:19) God "DNA's" us with His Presence and with the character of who He is, placing the very image of Himself in our spirits. Through the Holy Spirit we can enjoy sweet communion with God 24 hours a day!

The Marching Order Is Important

Even Judah's place in the "camping and marching order" of the 12 tribes of Israel in the Sinai desert was carefully directed by God for *our benefit*, as well as for that of the Jews! Yes, this provides a type and a shadow for our instruction today. Each day, the Israelites settled down for the night in a designated order surrounding the tabernacle, which was at the center of the camp. In other words, the *place of worship* was central to every aspect of their lives, awake or asleep! The tribe of Judah was situated right in front of the east gate of the tabernacle, the only entrance into the tabernacle, or God's Presence. There is no entry into the Kingdom of God and Heaven except through the Lion of Judah, Jesus Christ. There's more:

> **On the east side, toward the rising of the sun**, *those of the standard of the forces with **Judah** shall camp according to their armies; and Nahshon the son of Amminadab shall be the leader of the children of Judah. ... All who were numbered according to their armies of the forces with Judah, one hundred and eighty-six thousand four hundred—**these shall break camp first*** (Numbers 2:3,9).

In other words, Judah was always to lead the rest of the Israelites as they followed God by day and by night. Praise will lead the way in times of peace and also in times of war.

Warfare and Praise Are Connected

> *Praise the Lord! Sing to the Lord a new song, and His praise in the assembly of saints. Let Israel rejoice in their Maker; let the children of Zion be joyful in their King. Let them praise His name with the dance; let them sing praises to Him with the timbrel and harp. For the Lord takes pleasure in His people; He will beautify the humble with salvation. Let the saints be joyful in glory; let them sing aloud on their beds.*

Let the high praises of God be in their mouth, and a two-edged sword in their hand, to execute vengeance on the nations, and punishments on the peoples; to bind their kings with chains, and their nobles with fetters of iron; to execute on them the written judgment—this honor have all His saints. Praise the Lord! (Psalm 149)

The freer we get, the freer our churches will be! We have been the bound trying to set the bound free, and it just doesn't work. God is out to set His people free, and the principal weapon He has given His Church is praise and worship! One of the most amazing illustrations of this principle is found in Second Chronicles chapter 20 where King Jehoshaphat of Judah found himself in a tight spot. He was about to be attacked by not one, but three invading armies from Moab, Ammon, and Syria! He did what the Church needs to do more often: He proclaimed a time of fasting and prayer (see 2 Chron. 20:3). All Judah obeyed, and the communities and families of the nation came together for one single purpose before God.

Our Eyes Are Upon You

King Jehoshaphat, as the leader, set the tone for victory when he led a corporate prayer rehearsing God's faithfulness to Judah, and bluntly admitted the truth: "*...we have no power* against this great multitude that is coming against us; *nor do we know what to do,* but our eyes are upon You" (2 Chron. 20:12). God answered immediately by moving upon a Levite priest with a prophetic promise of deliverance! Before we move on, I want to point out that the deliverance of Judah didn't come through praise alone, nor through the fasting, or even through the unity of Judah.

It was the combination of all these ingredients together that released God to move on their behalf (we are back to cross-pollination again, you see).

One of the things that King Jehoshaphat said to the Lord is very interesting:

> *And now, here are the people of Ammon, Moab, and Mount Seir—whom **You would not let Israel invade when they came out of the land of Egypt, but they turned from them and did not destroy them**—here they are, rewarding us by coming to throw us out of Your possession which You have given us to inherit. O our God, will You not judge them?* (2 Chronicles 20:10-12a)

God had placed these invading nations in the promised land, and it wasn't King Jehoshaphat's place to destroy or fight against them. Listen to God's amazing answer: "Do not be afraid nor dismayed because of this great multitude, *for the battle is not yours, but God's*" (2 Chron. 20:15b).

I believe that the Church is moving into areas of warfare and conflict with principalities and powers that we must leave squarely in the hands of God. We are in a season where we will do what Moses told Israel to do at the shore of the Red Sea: "Stand still, and see the salvation of the Lord" (Ex. 14:13). Yes, He is telling us to put on our armor and the helmet of salvation. But once we have presented ourselves for battle, He wants us to watch His glory in action. God told King Jehoshaphat and Judah:

> *You will not need to fight in this battle. Position your-selves, stand still and see the salvation of the Lord, who is with you, O Judah and Jerusalem! Do not fear*

or be dismayed; tomorrow go out against them, for the Lord is with you (2 Chronicles 20:17).

The Biblical Posture of Desperation

What happened next is significant for the Church today. The Bible says King Jehoshaphat "bowed his head with his face to the ground, and all Judah and the inhabitants of Jerusalem bowed before the Lord, worshipping the Lord" (2 Chron. 20:18). This is a *biblical posture* for people who have seen God move in response to humble prayer and desperation. Some people have trouble with the deep bowing that they see in many renewal and revival meetings around the world, but God has *never* had a problem with it. When I visited Israel, I saw devout Jews bowing repeatedly before the wailing wall in reverent prayer and humility to God. I believe that is what Jehoshaphat was doing. The people of Judah had humbled themselves because they were in a tight spot and they knew it. America and most of the nations of the world are in a tight spot today, and we had better realize it. Our cities are in trouble, our families are in trouble, and our economies are in dire straits. It is time for us to stop playing church and become the Church, an anointed place of deliverance and a haven for the lost.

I wonder about the Levite priests, the sons of Asaph. How did they feel that morning when King Jehoshaphat lined them up and told them to go out and sing God's praises before the armies of their enemies? That had to take some faith! There had to be a tremendous anointing upon them, and they had to begin to see themselves in a different light. Those people weren't going to do their "three songs and a special." They weren't conducting a choir rehearsal. They had to get into the spirit and sing with all their being—their lives and the lives of Judah depended on it. Jehoshaphat's final word to them clinched the deal. He said, "Believe in the Lord your God, and you shall be established; believe His prophets, and you shall prosper" (2 Chron. 20:20b).

Now follow this Scripture passage carefully, because God Himself is about to write the "conclusion" to this chapter on praise in warfare:

> *And when he had consulted with the people,* **he** **appointed those who should sing to the Lord, and** **who should praise the beauty of holiness,** *as they* *went out before the army and were saying: "Praise* *the Lord, for His mercy endures forever." Now* **when** **they began to sing and to praise, the Lord set** **ambushes** *against the people of Ammon, Moab, and* *Mount Seir, who had come against Judah; and they* *were defeated* (2 Chronicles 20:21-22).

Set an "Ambush" of Praise and Worship

If you have eyes to see, then you have just seen God's prescription for warfare and total victory at the dawn of this season of incredible harvest! *Now when they began to sing* *and to praise, the Lord set ambushes....* I long to see churches of every denomination in every city come together to worship, praise, and pray to our Father in Heaven, enthroning Him as Supreme Lord over our cities and the nations. Am I naive? I think not. This is what God wants, and millions of believers are sensing this same deep longing well up in their spirits.

There are three final points that we must glean from this battle recorded in Second Chronicles chapter 20. First of all, King Jehoshaphat, the Levite singers and musicians, and the people of Judah *still needed faith* in God's promises to dance and sing when they knew three overwhelmingly large enemy armies were advancing toward them on the opposite side of a hill. Even though we are learning how to conduct spiritual warfare through worship and praise to God, it will still take *faith*.

Second, if the experience of the Israelites is an example for us today, then we probably won't be prepared for the results of our obedience to God in spiritual warfare.

So when Judah came to a place overlooking the wilderness, they looked toward the multitude; and there were their dead bodies, fallen on the earth. No one had escaped (2 Chronicles 20:24).

King Jehoshaphat and the people were shocked when they found their enemies' bodies lying on the ground. While they worshiped God, He arose and fought the battle on their behalf. He confounded their enemies and caused them to turn on one another in fatal conflict. This truth should be permanently sealed in our hearts and minds. The most effective thing that we can do in times of trouble, crisis, and conflict is to confess to the Lord, "We don't know what to do, but our eyes are still on You!" When we follow that up with worship and praise, God releases His unlimited power on our behalf.

Take Us to the Valley of Berachah

Third, when we worship and praise God in the middle of a valley of despair or crisis, we will inevitably cross over to *the valley of blessing*! That is exactly what happened to King Jehoshaphat and the people of Judah.

> *When Jehoshaphat and his people came to take away their spoil, they found among them an abundance of valuables on the dead bodies, and precious jewelry, which they stripped off for themselves, more than they could carry away; and they were three days gathering the spoil because there was so much. And on the fourth day they assembled in the Valley of Berachah, for there they blessed the Lord...* (2 Chronicles 20:25-26).

I believe God when He says that the wealth of the sinner is stored up for the righteous (see Prov. 13:22). The people of Judah named the valley where God had destroyed their enemies "the Valley of Berachah." The Hebrew word *berachah* means "benediction; prosperity, blessing."[4]

When we see the enemies and opposers of the Kingdom brought to self-destruction, when we see millions come to Jesus and the wealth of the sinner released into the work of the Kingdom of righteousness, it won't be because we strategized. It won't even happen because of anything we did. It will happen because we obeyed.

A Repentant Church Is a Changing Church

Obedience is *always* better than sacrifice, and God is trying to show the Church that through repentance there is great release of His power. He wants us to see that love flowing through the Church is *stronger* than hate flowing in the world. Unity in the Church is greater than dissimulation or discord. When we see what the enemy is doing in our churches, we tend to get overwhelmed. But what we need to do is rise up and let the Spirit of God come forth. When we let His unconditional love flow out of us, all bitterness and unforgiveness will be dealt with immediately. This is why the Lord has put such a strong emphasis on holiness and repentance in this move of His Spirit. A repentant Church is a changing Church that is open to the free movement and ministry of the Holy Spirit. A cleansed Church reflects the character of Christ rather than the character of the world, and as He is lifted up, He will draw all men unto Himself!

Renewal, revival, and the harvest have almost nothing to do with us. He is drawing us to Himself. It is His Spirit doing the work. It is not because all of a sudden we decided that we want to see revival, or see God show up in our services. It is by His Spirit. He is visiting the Church with His own Presence. He is arresting the Church, and He is revealing to us just how totally hopeless and helpless we are apart from Him. He is telling us to apply the salve of repentance to our eyes so that they can be opened to see what we are really like.

My final note on Second Chronicles chapter 20 is this: King Jehoshaphat and the people of Judah didn't stop worshiping and praising God once they had the victory and received financial blessing.

Then they returned, every man of Judah and Jerusalem, with Jehoshaphat in front of them, to go back to Jerusalem with joy, for the Lord had made them rejoice over their enemies. ***So they came to Jerusalem, with stringed instruments and harps and trumpets, to the house of the Lord.*** *And the fear of God was on all the kingdoms of those countries when they heard that the Lord had fought against the enemies of Israel. Then the realm of*

Jehoshaphat was quiet, for his God gave him rest all around (2 Chronicles 20:27-30).

Pray this prayer with me on behalf of your family, your local church body, your geographical location, and your nation:

Arise in our midst, O God. Take dominion, Lord. We turn loose of the reins and we say, "Lord, we cannot fight our own battles, but our eyes are on You." God, we give up; and Lord, we lean on You. Dear Lord, restore to the Church everything that the enemy has robbed and stolen from us and from our rightful inheritance. Restore true worship and praise to us, O God, so that we may worship You in spirit and in truth. Let Your Body rise up as a mighty army called to praise and worship in the earth, O God. Let God arise and our enemies be scattered. In Jesus' name we pray and give praise. Amen.

Endnotes

1.   This testimony to God's supernatural power was relayed to me by Dene Redmon in written form at my request at the time of this writing.

2.   James Strong, *Strong's Exhaustive Concordance of the Bible* (Peabody, Massachusetts: Hendrickson Publishers, n.d.), derived from definitions and root meanings for **Judah** (Hebrew, #3063).

3.   *Strong's*, **yada** (Hebrew, #3034).

4.   *Strong's*, **berachah** (Hebrew, #1294, 1293).

Chapter 6

Revealing the Heart

I have some good news and some bad news for you. The good news is that thanks to Jesus, who died and rose again for us, *everyone* can hear God's voice and discern His heart (not just an elite few). The bad news—at least until you understand God's principles of warfare—is that *He still puts His singers and worshipers in front* in times of battle!

That means that we still have to die to ourselves daily and step to the line of harm's way in times of spiritual warfare. But when we do, we do it with the full assurance of His love and authority in our hearts. Intimacy transports us light years beyond a mere mental understanding and consent to God's love and our salvation in Christ. Our intimate relationship brings the passion of His Presence into the equation of prayer and spiritual warfare. In His mercy and grace, God has chosen to *live in our hearts* through the great Comforter, who also guides and teaches us daily.

If this is true, then why do so many Christians still live like the Israelites did in the desert? Think about it. The

Israelites never heard God for themselves: They sent Moses to the mountain to hear God for them, and then he would deliver the condensed version to them once in a while. They didn't hold themselves personally accountable to God because they didn't *know* Him; they simply did their best to obey the laws they'd received from a third party. And they paid their "fines" (sin offerings) as needed each year. Anything else, anything disruptive or out of the usual order of things, was greeted with very little enthusiasm. They only thought about God in times of danger, hunger, or dissatisfaction. They quickly forgot about the good things they had seen and received, and they constantly focused on what they *didn't* have that particular day. They overlooked the fact that no one among them got sick and that their clothes never seemed to wear out for a 40-year period, but they were quick to complain about the food and to reminisce about how good it was "back in Egypt."

God Is Arresting Hearts for His Purposes

God has spoken to me prophetically to say, "In this day I am breaking into the hearts and lives of men. All walls must come down. For My Spirit is moving and continues to move in ways that you have not even considered, nor has entered into your hearts or minds. Therefore, it is necessary that your walls come down. For only in this manner shall My Spirit be able to arrest your hearts for My purposes. Your hearts are what I'm collecting. I am collecting the hearts of My people, and I will pour forth *from My heart into your heart*, and you shall be able to pour forth out of your hearts the love necessary to receive the lost. So open your hearts this day. Let your walls come down to receive from My throne and your lives and your hearts shall be changed for My purpose."

The next time you find yourself in an anointed atmosphere of corporate worship and praise, take a few moments to watch what happens spontaneously among the people around you. I can safely predict that you will see both tears and laughter, both repentance and rejoicing. You may even see some people bowing and others leaping; some kneeling and others sprawling on their faces before God. Some will sit quietly in their seats, while others will shout and cry out to God in loud voices (although they may be ushered out in some more restrictive church environments—but that's okay; the Holy Spirit will go out with them).

How can so many different (and seemingly opposite) expressions of human emotion and inward activity take place in the same meeting? God uses our worship and praise to supernaturally reveal what is in our hearts—regardless of what we see when He pulls away the veil or pulls down the walls obscuring our true selves. Much as extreme heat will bring impurities to the surface of a molten metal (the dross), God's Presence will bring to the surface anything that is displeasing to Him. This is always accompanied by a deep, pressing desire to repent and be made whole.

Let me rock your boat a little more by saying this: *God doesn't need our praise or worship.* No, I'm not stepping into heresy, I'm realigning our thinking to conform to God's Word. Yes, God *deserves*, *commands*, and *desires* our praise and worship, but He doesn't need it to be complete or whole in Himself. *We* are the ones in need and who benefit from giving Him the worship He deserves.

No Wonder It Feels So Good!

God is not on an ego trip, nor does He have self-worth problems or low self-esteem. He simply doesn't need our worship and praise to affirm His worth or supreme power. He is totally and utterly God with or without man's approval, worship, praise, or acknowledgment. Worship and praise is for us. It is for our mental, emotional, and spiritual health. When we worship God and praise Him, we have stepped back into the original purpose for which we were created and designed—*no wonder it feels so good*!

I have always said that people who are praisers and worshipers will not need to go to psychologists. Why? When we begin to worship, it makes us "outer-spective." When we begin to worship as David did, then no matter what our situation is, God begins to be expanded in our revelation. We begin to forget about our problems as they are minimized and made smaller and smaller in comparison to our Mighty God as our vision of Him gets greater and greater.

People who are worshipers and praisers don't have a lot of depression. How can you be depressed when you are intimately connected with God Almighty? When you begin, you may feel like a tiny speck of matter in relation to the expanse of the universe. But when you begin to see God's glory and worth, and understand how much He loves you and what He has made you—His own child—everything changes. Once your status as a beloved child of God gets down into your spirit and becomes revelation knowledge, you will be lifted higher and higher. You begin to understand that God meant what He said when He said,

The steps of a good man are ordered by the Lord, and He delights in his way. Though he fall, he shall not be

utterly cast down; for the Lord upholds him with His hand (Psalm 37:23-24).

When we begin to see who we are in God and what great plans He has for us, depression loses its footing and falls away from our lives.

Intercession Requires Intimacy

We can have no prayer life without a relationship with Jesus Christ. Intercession, in particular, is first and foremost a matter of intimacy and relationship with Jesus. He wants your fellowship. He wants to enjoy a renewed relationship with *you*, personally. That's what this "Christian thing" is all about: relationship. It is not about doctrine, although that is important. It's not about fellowship, although that is important. It is about relationship. Without a personal relationship and intimacy with the Lord, a person's prayer life will be dead. It will be reduced to dead works, and he or she will be no different than the Pharisees and the Sadduccees. That person will be *performing* Christianity rather than *living* Christianity.

It is through praise and worship that Jesus arrests our hearts and draws us into His Presence. Each week many people come to Brownsville Assembly of God seeking revival. The word of the Lord to us today is, "Don't seek revival—seek Me." Your hope and desire may be to light the fires of revival in your congregation or church body, and it is true that the drier the wood is, the faster it burns. If your purpose is to start revival, then you need to back up. You need to know that revival can be in your heart whether it is in your congregation or not. That's where it must start. Revival starts through relationship.

We have preferred the "easy-believism" of "give me" religion because we have been seeking His hand instead of His face. God is speaking in the midst of the Church today, saying, "Seek My face." Are we too blind to see that His hand automatically comes with His face? Jesus told us not to be concerned about what we are going to wear or eat. He said, "But seek first the kingdom of God and His righteousness, and all these things shall be added to you" (Mt. 6:33).

We have been going around rebuking the devil, binding and loosing, and all that stuff, and that's good. There's a place for all that. But sometimes satan's name is mentioned more in a church service than those of Jesus and the Holy Spirit. The Lord wants us to get back to basics: the worship and the praise. I believe that we enthrone Him with our worship and our praise. Jesus said, "And I, if I am lifted up from the earth, will draw all peoples to Myself" (Jn. 12:32).

We need to establish a New Testament truth using an Old Testament type and shadow:

> *Coming to Him as to a living stone, rejected indeed by men, but chosen by God and precious, you also, as living stones, are being built up a spiritual house, **a holy priesthood**, to offer up **spiritual sacrifices** acceptable to God through Jesus Christ. ... But you are a chosen generation, a royal priesthood, a holy nation, His own special people, **that you may proclaim the praises of Him who called you** out of darkness into His marvelous light; who once were not a people but are now the people of God, who had not obtained mercy but now have obtained mercy* (1 Peter 2:4-5,9-10).

The Old Testament type and shadow of the reality described in First Peter chapter 2 is the Aaronic priesthood that Moses established at God's command. The Bible tells us that all the things that happened to the children of Israel in the wilderness are a pattern or example for us (see 1 Cor. 10:5-12). This assumes, of course, that we will be bright enough to discern the difference between their mistakes and their correct choices.

First Minister to God
(Then He'll Tell You How to Minister to People)

God told Moses, "Now take Aaron your brother, and his sons with him, from among the children of Israel, *that he may minister to Me* as priest..." (Ex. 28:1). Aaron did not minister to Moses or to the Israelites—he ministered to God. As kings and priests in the Messianic priesthood, our first and foremost purpose in the Kingdom of God is to *minister to God*. The Old Testament priest was also an intercessor, who was to stand before God and intercede for the people. *As we minister* to the Lord under the new covenant of grace, He gives us instructions on how to minister to man (our secondary purpose).

According to John, Jesus Christ was the Word (the *Logos*) made flesh. He spoke the worlds into existence (see Jn. 1:3,14; Heb. 11:3). God establishes things with His Word, and that is why prayer is so important. God knows what we need to pray about, but He wants *you and I* to speak it out. That, in turn, sets something in motion and creates a reality in the earth. The Old Testament pattern was, "First the natural, then the spiritual" (see 1 Cor. 15:46). God created a lifeless human body from the soil of the garden of

Eden. Then He breathed His own life into the body, and Adam was a living being.

The New Testament pattern reverses the curse and everything else as well: "First the spiritual, then the natural." When we are born again, we are made new creatures and everything becomes new (see 2 Cor. 5:17) — except our bodies and the earth around us. They will be redeemed later. When God was ready to release the river of His Spirit over the earth, He began to move on His people to hunger and thirst for Him as never before. He caused them to pray and praise in ways they had never dreamed, then He suddenly descended on them and revealed His glory. First the spiritual, then the natural.

The heavens are being seeded right now with intercession for the harvest. I can confidently tell you that the *first harvest* that you will see in your church *will not be what you are planting right now*. Your first harvest will come *where somebody else has already planted* before you, where somebody else has already watered. Do you remember the evangelist Tommy Hicks? When he came to Argentina in 1954, he came in and reaped where he hadn't sown. That wasn't wrong—it was God! When the second great revival came to Argentina in 1982, beginning with a crusade conducted by businessman Carlos Annacondia in La Plata, Argentina, that resulted in 40,000 people coming to Jesus, it was clear that Brother Carlos was also reaping where others had faithfully sown before him. The same is true of the rivers of renewal and revival that have flooded Toronto, Canada; Sunderland and London, England; and Pensacola, Florida.

The only way true revival reaps a *continual* harvest is for there to be *continual intercession* and obedience to every direction of God. That is why Pastor John Kilpatrick has felt it so vital for us to intercede for the harvest every night of revival in Brownsville. It makes sense. We need to keep sowing, watering, and reaping if we expect to continue reaping a harvest.

There was one piece of furniture in the Old Testament tabernacle (and later in the temples) that was exclusively dedicated to worship: the golden altar of incense. The high priest was required to offer incense on this altar at the time of the morning and the evening sacrifice *perpetually*. This was different from the sacrifices that had to do with the needs of mankind. The incense offered on the altar of incense was devoted exclusively to God, for His own benefit, pleasure, and enjoyment. This is also the first priority of prophetic intercession. We minister first to the Lord, and then we allow Him to tell us if, when, and how we will minister in prayer for the needs of people at that particular time.

According to Exodus 30:1-8, the golden altar of incense was placed right in front of the veil that separated the holy place from the ark of the Testimony in the Holy of Holies (according to *Strong's Concordance*, the ark of the Testimony may literally be translated as "ark of the Prince"[1]). Our predominant position as priests ministering to the Lord is at the altar of incense—only now the veil of separation has been totally removed. As we offer the incense of worship and praise to God and His Prince of Peace, we are face-to-face with His Presence and glory!

The Psalmist wrote, "Let my *prayer* be set before You as *incense*, the *lifting up of my hands* as the *evening sacrifice*"

(Ps. 141:2). We need to keep this spiritual perspective in mind. The Hebrew word for incense, *qetoreth*, literally means "to fumigate."[2] This helps explain why so many are coming to understand that warfare through worship and praise is carrying the spiritual conflict to a "higher level" than in the level of the second heaven where we find principalities, powers, and rulers of darkness gathered. Praise and worship transports us directly into the Presence of God in the Holy of Holies, or throne room. God wants to bring the entire Church into this higher level today, but it will only happen when we begin to minister directly to *Him* before the altar of incense (worship), seeking His face instead of His hand. It is when we minister to Him that He meets with us at the Mercy Seat of Christ (see Ex. 30:6).

When we offer God the incense of our unrestrained worship and praise, He will release His Shekinah glory and Presence among us. That in turn begins to "fumigate" the heavens around us! His glory drives out all the "critters and the creeping, crawling things" that the enemy would send into our lives. Praise and worship actually begins to *transform us* and it opens our eyes so that we can see the powers of darkness pushed back in every area that God fumigates in us as well. Yes, our praise and worship cleanses *us* even as we offer it to God! As the Church is beginning to catch the vision for anointed praise and worship to the Lord, He is "fumigating" our churches, cities, and nations through the worship and praise as well.

Two Responses: Burning Roasts or Burning Hearts

Obedience always seem to come at a cost. Expect some problems when you begin to increase your investment in true praise and worship. First, you will probably hear from

the people who have roasts burning in their ovens and tem-
pers flaring in your services. They want "three songs and a
special" as usual, and they expect God (and you) to get busy
so that they can be out of church promptly by 11:30 a.m.
They'll let Jesus heal on the sabbath or on Sundays—but
only as long as He is quick about it.

You will also begin to see something marvelous happen
in the house of God and in your community. As you begin
to put God first by making praise and worship your primary
priority, you will see people being transformed as they enter
the Presence of the Lord. Almost immediately, their prayer
life will begin to change too—without pressure from the
pulpit or a 14-week teaching on the efficacy of prayer. They
will instinctively begin to move into prophetic intercession
and the deep places of God. Then you will see them
immersed in a new passion from God for the lost. Suddenly
you'll see your ministry spill out into the streets!

You just can't stand to keep this to yourself when God
breaks your heart for the lost. (That is exactly what happened to the congregation at Brownsville Assembly of God.
When God's Presence hit the people, they discovered that
they couldn't pray like they used to anymore.) Your hearts
will begin to bleed out into your neighborhoods and into the
city! You won't be content anymore with church as usual.
Forget the usual schedule; you will be faced with a strong
passion to go out and feed the hungry in Jesus' name. You
will want to go down to the ghetto to pray for the drug
addicts to set them free. You will want to go to the schools
and see the young people touched by the power of God.
Your heart will bleed out into the street in the same way that
Jesus took His earthly ministry "to the streets."

Consider what happened when the "sinful woman" brought her alabaster box of praise and worship for Jesus into a Pharisee's house. Both hell and Heaven broke loose at the same time! According to the Gospel record that begins in Luke 7:36, a sinful woman entered the house of Simon, a Pharisee, who had invited Jesus into his home for a meal. When this woman broke open her box of expensive perfume and began to weep and bathe the feet of Jesus with her tears and the perfume, three things manifested themselves immediately.

First, the beautiful fragrance of the woman's brokenness came forth and touched the Son of God's heart, and she was totally forgiven of her sins. Second, the *very same act* revealed the twisted heart of the Pharisee, Simon. He began to echo the words of satan during the temptation of Christ when he said, "This Man, *if* He were a prophet, would know who and what manner of woman this is who is touching Him, for she is a sinner" (Lk. 7:39b). Genuine worship and praise turns up the heat of God's glory and brings to the surface whatever is hidden from view. Third, the heart of God was revealed to all who had eyes to see and ears to hear:

> *"Therefore I say to you, **her sins, which are many, are forgiven, for she loved much.** But to whom little is forgiven, the same loves little." Then He said to her, "Your sins are forgiven"* (Luke 7:47-48).

We are going to see the sinner's heart touched through worship and praise as never before! It is already happening. When we began to adopt more worship and praise in our intercession at Brownsville (and less binding and loosing), *we immediately began to see the number of souls coming to Christ increase in the services*! I challenge you to explain it.

I know I don't understand it, but then there are a lot of things I don't understand about our mighty God and His Kingdom. The miracle of salvation may be the greatest mystery in the universe. I always say that what took one second down at the altar has taken me my entire life to begin to understand!

We see this revelation of hearts throughout the New Testament. In the story of the prodigal son, once the wayward son returned to his father in repentance, the father declared a feast, and they began to be merry and rejoice (a picture of praise and worship over the restoration of something precious). The wayward son's heart of brokenness and repentance was clearly apparent to everyone, and at the same time, the jealous and spiteful heart of the "good" elder son exploded into the open in Luke 15:29-30. His comments perfectly echo the claims of offended, self-righteous Pharisees who have often claimed to have kept all God's commandments and are offended to see sinners freely forgiven (without the works of the flesh) and accepted in God's favor without shame. The father's words reflect the heart of God toward both kinds of sons.

If you are a pastor, then don't be surprised if most of your "people" problems rise up in your worship department! Why? Because the enemy knows that is where the praise and worship is. He'll battle your worship team up one side and down the other. Everything that is hidden will come out. You'll have civil wars in your worship department, but keep pointing them to Jesus Christ, and they'll win (and the church body will win too). *God cleans a house so He can bless and heal in that house!*

> *Then Jesus went into the temple of God and drove out
> all those who bought and sold in the temple, and
> overturned the tables of the money changers and the
> seats of those who sold doves. And He said to them,
> "It is written, 'My house shall be called a house of
> prayer,' but you have made it a 'den of thieves.' "*
> **Then the blind and the lame came** *to Him in the
> temple,* **and He healed them** (Matthew 21:12-14).

The devil knows that if the Church ever begins to get a
hold of this truth, he will be on his way out. When Jesus
went into the house of God and drove out all the darkness,
the blind and the lame came to Him and He healed them. In
other words, *when Jesus cleaned out the Church, people
started getting saved and healed, and the blind began to
see*! Let that one settle in.

It doesn't end there. Remember, praise and worship
reveals hearts. When the chief priests of the temple heard
the voices of children crying out in worship, "Hosanna to
the Son of David," and saw the wonderful things Jesus had
done, they were indignant (see Mt. 21:15). When they
pointed out what the children were saying, Jesus said something that we need to take to heart ourselves: "Have you
never read, 'Out of the mouth of babes and nursing infants
You have perfected praise'?" (Mt. 21:16b)

The children's praises to God revealed the religious spirit at work in those Pharisees. That same spirit of religion is
influencing many people in the Church today too! You may
say, "The Christian doesn't have a spirit of religion." Get
real, folks. Of all the powers of darkness, the spirit of religion may well be one of the greatest. The Church has
focused most of its attention on pornography shops, and

yes, the enemy is at work there. But these visible manifestations of evil are the lowest order of the demonic realm. The highest orders are those spirits with the power to transform themselves "into angels of light," hiding themselves behind the cloak of "respectability," meanwhile manipulating and controlling the flow of political power and money and religion. Yes, I said "religion."

Satan is very religious. *I didn't say satan was spiritual,* and I didn't say he was Christian. I said he is *religious.* He can quote the Scriptures like a seminary professor while dragging a human soul to hell—but he can't stand the searing pain of the holiness of the Presence of the living God. If you ever have trouble discerning whether a "voice" is from God or not, just start praising and worshiping God. Your confusion will end in seconds. Praise and worship reveals hearts.

> *Then, as He* [Jesus] *was now drawing near the descent of the Mount of Olives, the whole multitude of the disciples began to rejoice and praise God with a loud voice for all the mighty works they had seen, saying: "'Blessed is the King who comes in the name of the Lord!' Peace in heaven and glory in the highest!" And some of the Pharisees called to Him from the crowd, "Teacher, rebuke Your disciples." But He answered and said to them, "I tell you that if these should keep silent, the stones would immediately cry out"* (Luke 19:37-40).

In this passage, the Pharisees were, once again, offended by the worship and praise being offered to the Son of God, and it *revealed their heart.* This passage is followed by one of the saddest Scripture verses in the Bible. Jesus looked at the ancient city of Jerusalem and cried as He said, "If you had known, even you, especially in this your day, the things that make for your peace! But *now they are hidden from your eyes*" (Lk. 19:42).

Need Peace? Praise and Worship God!

The more time you spend in worship and praise, the more peaceful your life will be. This truth is perfectly pictured in the confrontation between King David and his wife, Michal, over public worship. When King David was finally able to bring the ark of the covenant into Jerusalem, he personally led a procession offering exuberant praise and worship to God. He became totally lost and absorbed in his devotion to God, and the two hearts were instantly revealed to be in stark contrast! David's heart was plainly revealed to everyone there—he "danced before the Lord with all his might" (2 Sam. 6:14). His wife Michal, on the other hand, "...looked through a window and saw King David leaping and whirling before the Lord; and *she despised him* in her heart" (2 Sam. 6:16). When praise and worship became the order of the day in Jerusalem, *David came in to bless* and *Michal went out to criticize* (see 2 Sam. 6:20). Some things never change.

I love David's answer. Various versions of it have become the watchword of this mighty move of God across the earth: "I *will* play music before the Lord. And I will be *even more undignified than this* and *will be humble* in my own sight" (2 Sam. 6:21b-22a). The verse that follows should be a solemn warning to any of us who feel an "anointing to criticize" coming on: "Therefore Michal the daughter of Saul had no children to the day of her death" (2 Sam. 6:23). She became barren in the things of the natural and the spirit because she despised the unrestrained praise and worship her husband offered to the Lord.

The complementary truths of spiritual warfare and praise and worship are perfectly "married" together in Psalm 149. Again, I want to allow God Himself to conclude this chapter with His Word:

> *Praise the Lord! Sing to the Lord a new song, and His praise in the assembly of saints. Let Israel rejoice in their Maker; let the children of Zion be joyful in their King. Let them praise His name with the dance; let them sing praises to Him with the timbrel and harp. For the Lord takes pleasure in His people; He will beautify the humble with salvation. Let the saints be joyful in glory; let them sing aloud on their beds. **Let the high praises of God be in their mouth, and a two-edged sword in their hand**, to execute vengeance on the nations, and punishments on the peoples; **to bind their kings with chains, and their nobles with fetters of iron**; to execute on them the written judgment—this honor have all His saints. Praise the Lord!* (Psalm 149)

Endnotes

1.   James Strong, *Strong's Exhaustive Concordance of the Bible* (Peabody, Massachusetts: Hendrickson Publishers, n.d.), **testimony** (Hebrew, #5715, 5707, 5749).

2.   *Strong's*, **incense** (Hebrew, #7004).

Chapter 7

The Sword of the Lord

The Lord of the harvest is examining the fruit. He's cutting away all unfruitfulness. What God is doing is more than a revival. It's more than a renewal. He's getting the Church ready for His glory. Others may look at us and say, "I see fruit," but God sees the true fruit. He's asking the Church to begin to display the fruit of the Spirit, not only to one another, but to the world. If we are fruitful, then we will be able to bring in the harvest. It's an unusual day.

The Lord has been dealing with us about intercession for several years, but recently He also began to teach us about His sword and our tongues. They are all linked together. He wants the Church to begin to speak words of blessing, not curses. We have spoken curses into our own lives, we've spoken curses into the lives of our family, we've spoken curses into our churches, we've spoken curses into our cities, and God wants the Church to begin to speak blessing. Why? Because it is in blessing that the power of God will begin to be released.

I believe that there is a new level of anointing for the prophetic that will be simply awesome and powerful. It will be a whole new realm that the Church hasn't seen since the first century, *if then*. He is conditioning us to be able to speak words of power that will set the captive free. He will make our words sharper than a two-edged sword. These will be words of destruction, if they are misused, but words of blessing, glory, and life if we speak them by the dictates of the Spirit. When I first received the understanding of this message, the Presence of the Lord was so tangible that I knew this was an urgent and timely word that *must be delivered* to God's people.

Less than six months before this writing, Brother Randy Clark preached a message entitled, "The Making of a Warrior" at Toronto Airport Christian Fellowship (TACF) on the third anniversary of the outpouring of God's Spirit there. When Brother Randy announced the title of his message, the Spirit of the Lord fell powerfully on a number of people in the meeting, and especially on Carol Arnott, who fell to the floor. (Carol is co-pastor of TACF with her husband, John.)

For almost 20 minutes while she lay on the floor, Carol appeared to be slashing violently at something, almost as if she held a "double-edged broadsword" in her clasped hands. (At this point in the book, you probably understand that Carol had dropped into prophetic intercession, and God was illustrating something in the spirit realm using her physical body.) After Randy Clark finished his message, Carol got up and powerfully delivered this prophecy that has since been distributed around the world:

"This is My sword, this is not man's sword, this is My golden sword. The ways you have been using My weapons, the methods that you have been using in the past, you are to throw them away because I am giving you My sword now and the old ways of doing things will not do. The old methods will not be acceptable to Me anymore because I am doing a new thing.

"Do not look to the yesterdays but look to the future because I am doing a new thing and this new way is not the old. This new way is new and you must throw away the old ways of doing things and take up My sword because My sword is made of pure gold and is purer and is mighty.

"If you wield it the captives will be set free, the chains will be broken and the healings will be manifest because it will not be by might, nor by power, but by My wonderful Holy Spirit. It is by Him, it is by Him that this new wave will be brought forth, it is by Him that the King of Kings and Lord of Lords will ride again.

"In this next wave I am requiring those who take up this golden sword to be refined, to be pure, to have all the dross refined in the fire because if you take this sword and there is secret sin in your life, *this sword will kill you*. This next wave is no joke. It is not a laughing matter. All those who do not want to give up their sin and are fearful, like Gideon's men, stand back, because I am calling men and women in these next days that will allow Me to refine them, that will allow Me to chasten, but not with anger because I am a loving God. I am a God full of mercy but I am serious as the time is short.

"The bridegroom is most anxious for His bride, so those of you that will, let Me refine you and come and take up that golden sword for I will use you in ways, I will use you in ways that you can't imagine, but I must purify you first."[1]

Why is God sending repentance to the Church? Because He wants to equip the Church with newer and more complete understanding of His ancient tools. His Word has always been unchanging, but in this day, He is placing it in the mouths and hands of *purified and sanctified vessels* tried in the fires of holiness.

There is only one way to get the dross, or impurities, out of our lives, and that is through trials, tribulations, and pressure. If you haven't heard, this renewal and revival has encountered and overcome its fair share of trials, tribulations, and pressure. Some of the fire has come from within the Church, and some has come from without. Sometimes it has taken the form of criticism and verbal persecution, and at certain times and places it has taken the form of physical sickness and accidents. (Pastor John Kilpatrick at Brownsville suffered serious injuries on the same weekend that a number of other people were injured and a child in the church was killed.) We've even seen outright physical attacks and martyrdom occur for the gospel's sake (as in the case of Pastor Julio Cesar Ruibal, a prominent revival and prayer leader in South America who was gunned down in Cali, Colombia, on December 13, 1996, after receiving death threats because of his bold ministry in the heart of a territory dominated by drug lords[2]).

So if you are feeling pressure, that's good news. We are seeking His face in the midst of everything that is going on, and the solution is to seek His face like never before! If you recall the three (I've expanded them to the four) steps of intercession outlined by Reese Howell, worship draws us into *intimacy* with God. It is in this intimate atmosphere that we begin to sense and feel what God feels. It is here that we are led by the Spirit to *identify* with the purpose of God in the problems, the pain, and the pressures in the lives of other people in His Kingdom. This identity progresses until we begin to shoulder the burden of our brothers and sisters and so experience the *agony* they feel in their crisis or challenge.

Having denied our natural urge to see to our *own hurts, needs,* and *fears*; having taken up the cross on behalf of others at the bidding of Jesus; we begin to share His *authority* to address that problem in His name and power. This kind of prayer—uttered from within the Most Holy Place of His Presence, inspired by His Spirit within us, and totally in line with God's heart—is always answered. It is the God-ordained process of praying, "Your kingdom come. Your will be done *on earth* as it is in heaven" (Mt. 6:10).

The Old and New Testaments are full of instances where trials and tribulations worked wonderful perfection in people's lives. I am not saying that we must submit to the devil. If the devil sends something your way, rebuke it, bind it, and get rid of it. But we *must* submit to God's dealings in our lives. He is sending the fire of His Presence into the Church to perfect the gold in our lives while bringing the dross, or the impurities, to the top so that they can be removed.

I believe that God wants to release the prophetic into the Church, and intercession is very prophetic by nature. It assumes that we are able and equipped to hear God speak. Let me repeat that for emphasis. Intercession—especially prophetic intercession—assumes that we are able and equipped to hear God speak. If you aren't sure about this, let me assure you that we—and you, in particular—can do just that. My witness for that is no less than Jesus Christ who said, "And other sheep I have which are not of this fold; them also I must bring, *and they will hear My voice*; and there will be one flock and one shepherd" (Jn. 10:16); and *"My sheep hear My voice*, and I know them, and they follow Me" (Jn. 10:27).

God can speak to us through His Word, through dreams, visions, and gentle inward impressions, through other people, through the gifts of the Spirit, and through prophetic ministry in general. He has thoroughly equipped the Church with the ability to hear His voice by the Holy Spirit. There's a new sound coming, and if we are bowed down with the weight of religious tradition, we may very well miss God. We could miss Him completely if we are expecting Him to move only in a certain way. I firmly believe God will offend our minds to reveal our hearts.

God will release a corporate anointing to the Body of Christ in the days to come. The anointing will no longer be reserved for the pastor alone, or exclusively for the prophet or the apostle. In fact, it was *never* meant to be reserved this way. It was to be distributed throughout the Body of Christ, which, in turn, was to be equipped by the leadership gifts "for the work of the ministry." God is simply restoring us back to His original intent for the Church! He wants the entire Body of Christ to go out into the world and do great exploits in His name to His glory.

For the word of God is living and powerful, and sharper than any two-edged sword, piercing even to the division of soul and spirit, and of joints and marrow, and is a discerner of the thoughts and intents of the heart (Hebrews 4:12).

God is dividing our thoughts from the intents of the heart. He is separating the things of the flesh from the things of the spirit, and that's why it's so painful. He describes His Word as a "two-edged sword" that can turn any direction. He's doing this for a very specific reason. He wants us to pray what is *His will*, and about that which He wants us to pray. Much of the time we pray our own will, our own desires, and our own agenda. He wants us to understand that the words we speak—whether negative or positive—are powerful. The Church needs to begin speaking blessings.

The "sword of the Lord" shows up throughout the Bible:

He had in His right hand seven stars, out of His mouth went a sharp two-edged sword, and His countenance was like the sun shining in its strength (Revelation 1:16).

And to the angel of the church in Pergamos write, "These things says He who has the sharp two-edged sword" (Revelation 2:12).

Now I saw heaven opened, and behold, a white horse. And He who sat on him was called Faithful and True, and in righteousness He judges and makes war. His eyes were like a flame of fire, and on His head were many crowns. He had a name written that no one knew except Himself. He was clothed with a robe dipped in blood, and His name is called The

Word of God. And the armies in heaven, clothed in fine linen, white and clean, followed Him on white horses. Now out of His mouth goes a sharp sword, that with it He should strike the nations. And He Himself will rule them with a rod of iron. He Himself treads the winepress of the fierceness and wrath of Almighty God. And He has on His robe and on His thigh a name written: KING OF KINGS AND LORD OF LORDS. ... And I saw the beast, the kings of the earth, and their armies, gathered together to make war against Him who sat on the horse and against His army. Then the beast was captured, and with him the false prophet who worked signs in his presence, by which he deceived those who received the mark of the beast and those who worshiped his image. These two were cast alive into the lake of fire burning with brimstone. And the rest were killed with the sword which proceeded from the mouth of Him who sat on the horse. And all the birds were filled with their flesh (Revelation 19:11-16,19-21).

Regardless of our respective views of end-time prophecy, we can agree that God's Word exhibits a divine fierceness concerning the judgment that's coming on the kingdom of darkness, and we can agree that Scripture tells us it will come "...with the sword which proceeded from the mouth of Him [Jesus Christ] who sat on the horse..." (Rev. 19:21). My intention here isn't to delve into the mysteries of the endtimes; it is to establish that Jesus Christ is the source of the sword. His words need to be in our mouths because, according to God's Word, "...the testimony of Jesus is the spirit of prophecy" (Rev. 19:10b).

To illustrate the "two-edged" cutting nature of the Word, we turn to the words of Jesus in Luke 19:22 where He warned through the master's words to the unprofitable servant in the parable of the talents, "Out of your own mouth I will judge you...." Elsewhere we are told:

For out of the abundance of the heart the mouth speaks. A good man out of the good treasure of his heart brings forth good things, and an evil man out of the evil treasure brings forth evil things. But I say to you that for every idle word men may speak, they will give account of it in the day of judgment (Matthew 12:34b-36).

God is inspecting our fruit today. He has deposited precious gifts, abilities, and callings in us, and harvesttime is near—for souls *and for fruit*! We need to be about our Father's business. His Presence and glory are so holy that they will create a tremendous godly "fear" or awe in God's people. We will be afraid to speak anything except what He places in our mouths, and it will be for our own safety.

When Adam and Eve sinned in the garden of Eden, God did something for their own safety. In Genesis 3, we overhear a divine conversation and pronouncement:

Then the Lord God said, "Behold, the man has become like one of Us, to know good and evil. And now, lest he put out his hand and take also of the tree of life, and eat, and live forever"—therefore the Lord God sent him out of the garden of Eden to till the ground from which he was taken. So He drove out the man; and He placed cherubim at the east of the garden of Eden, **and a flaming sword which turned** *every way, to guard the way to the tree of life* (Genesis 3:22-24).

I believe that flaming sword represents the Word of God, the sword of life. One of the things the Lord has taught me is that the *entrance* into the Presence of God is also the key to hearing His voice. When sin polluted God's supreme creations, making it impossible for Him to dwell in their midst without His glory destroying them, He placed the cherubim at the *east gate* with the *flaming sword* to guard it.

Therefore it is no accident that the *gate* to His Presence in every type and shadow leading to the cross was always the *eastern gate,* and that these were always linked directly with the Law of Moses, the Levitical Law, and the Living Word, Jesus Christ. The Messiah is to reenter Jerusalem through the *eastern* gate. The only entrance to the Holy of Holies (and His manifest Presence—the Way, the Truth, and the Life) in the tabernacle of Moses, the temple of Solomon, and the temple of Herod, respectively, always faced the *east*.

The triumph of Jesus Christ on the cross made it possible for the veil of separation to be split from top to bottom, providing eternal access to God's Presence for those who are washed in the blood of the Lamb. Now it is our privilege to approach His Presence in intimate fellowship once again. But we must still approach Him only through the flaming sword of His Living Word, Jesus Christ. There is no other way to come to eternal life in God. It is highly significant to me that the images of the cherubim were woven into the veil of the temple separating the Holy Place from the Most Holy Place. When the veil was torn apart by God, the cherubim were symbolically "moved aside," as if God was reopening the eastern gate to the Tree of Life, Jesus Christ. This is the reverse of the curse, so to speak. Man was put out of the garden through the first Adam's sin, but at Calvary, man was given free access into the garden again through the sacrificial death of the sinless second Adam.

So where does the sword fit in? Inside the ark of the covenant, situated underneath the outstretched wings of the cherubim and the mercy seat, were the tablets of the law, God's Word. *This is the sword of the Lord*, which was contained in the innermost part of God's temple. God found a place where He could dwell *in the midst* of His people. This ties in perfectly with the passage that says, "*Your word* I have *hidden in my heart*, that I might not sin against You!" (Ps. 119:11)

The sword of the Lord is a "two-edged" sword. In other words, it cuts *both ways*. It can be used against enemies, and it can be used against friends and family members. It can bring protection and deliverance, or it can bring self-inflicted wounds or even death. When the cherubim were moved aside and mankind was given free access to God's Presence, the flaming sword was placed in our hearts. One of the most powerful prophecies of old concerned what would happen to the Word or Law of God when the Messiah would come:

> *But this is the covenant that I will make with the house of Israel after those days, says the Lord:* **I will put My law in their minds, and write it on their hearts;** *and I will be their God, and they shall be My people.* *No more shall every man teach his neighbor, and every man his brother, saying, "Know the Lord," for they all shall know Me, from the least of them to the greatest of them, says the Lord. For I will forgive*

their iniquity, and their sin I will remember no more
(Jeremiah 31:33-34).

The Holy of Holies, the dwelling place of God's
Presence, is now dwelling in our spirit, housed in the temple
of the Holy Ghost (our bodies). You and I live in a body, we
have a soul, and we are eternal spirits. Just as the tabernacle
and temples were divided into the outer court, the Holy
Place, and the Holiest of Holies; you and I have an outer
court called our body, an inner court called our soul (which
includes the mind, the intellect, the personality, soul, and
will), and a Holiest of Holies, our spirit. It is here where we
are born again. It is in the Holy Place, the soul, that renewal
must continually take place through the washing of the water
of the Word of God. It is in the body that sacrifices are continually offered as the old man of the flesh is crucified daily.

Too many of us in the Church are using the sword of
God's Word to curse our brethren, as the prophet Balaam
tried to do. As Carol Arnott's prophecy graphically points
out, we will not get away with it anymore. If we cut others
with our tongue, the two-edged sword of God's Word will
cut us!

You probably know the story of Balaam, the Mes-
opotamian "prophet for hire" who was approached by the
Moabites and asked to curse the people of God. Balak, the
king of the Moabites, told Balaam, "...curse this people
for me, for they are too mighty for me. Perhaps I shall be
able to defeat them and drive them out of the land, for I
know that he whom you bless is blessed, and he whom
you curse is cursed" (Num. 22:6). Balaam prays, and God
tells the prophet to go ahead but to do only what He spoke
to him (Num. 22:20). He sets a trap for this unrighteous

prophet whose words have power, but whose life is totally out of line.

The Bible says that Balaam's donkey had more discernment than this foolish prophet. The donkey saw the angel of the Lord blocking a narrow passage in the road, with his strong sword in his hand. When the wise donkey turned aside, her foolish master struck the donkey, but she still wouldn't move. Finally, God spoke to the "great prophet of God" through a donkey. (Sometimes "it takes one to reach one.") This is a prophetic picture of the narrow places to which the Lord is bringing His prophets today! The two-edged sword of the Lord awaits them, with an angelic warning: "Every word that proceeds from your mouth has to be placed there by the Lord, because the sword *cuts both ways*." (If you are a prophet, are your knees starting to knock?)

The Book of Proverbs says, "Death and life are in the power of the tongue, and those who love it will eat its fruit" (Prov. 18:21). We have been transformed into images of our Master—the same Master seen by John the apostle in the Revelation: "He had in His right hand seven stars, out of His mouth went a sharp two-edged sword, and His countenance was like the sun shining in its strength" (Rev. 1:16). (Carol Arnott was right.)

Too many of us in the Church are living on the edge of judgment because we have failed to control our tongues. We speak sharp, cutting words thoughtlessly, but God is saying the sword cuts both ways. We have made our *brethren* feel like David, who cried out to God, "My soul is among lions; I lie among the sons of men who are set on fire, whose teeth are spears and arrows, *and their tongue a sharp sword"* (Ps. 57:4). We need to remember that God hears every word, and He stores up every righteous prayer. Somehow I don't think explanations and justifications will do when we stand before Him. He demands righteousness. And He's demanding it *right now.*

The Book of Proverbs gives us another picture of the tongue:

> *He who speaks truth declares righteousness, but a false witness, deceit. There is one who speaks like the piercings of a sword, **but the tongue of the wise promotes health*** (Proverbs 12:17-18).

God is going to use your tongue to speak healing in people's lives, not only emotional or spiritual healing, but physical healing too! It will be the day of the sanctified tongue, of the Word being released through the mouths of God's people!

We will be held accountable for our words, just as Ananias and Sapphira were judged for their words before the Lord (see Acts 5:1-11). He simply won't put up with untruthfulness in His people—the stakes are too high. This is the season of harvest, when every hand is needed to bring in the harvest. It is a time for foolishness, laziness, and apathy to be put aside. It is a time for truth and right speaking to be the rule in the Church instead of the exception to the rule.

It is time for every blood-washed disciple of Jesus to declare the truth of Isaiah 49 as their own call to action today:

> *Listen, O coastlands, to Me, and take heed, you peoples from afar! The Lord has called Me from the*

womb; from the matrix of My mother He has made mention of My name. And He has made My mouth like a sharp sword; in the shadow of His hand He has hidden Me, and made Me a polished shaft; in His quiver He has hidden Me (Isaiah 49:1-2).

God has pulled us out of His quiver, the Church. It is time for war, but in a new way for a new day. The prophetic word in this harvest will be sharp. He is honing His sword in your life so that it can come out of your mouth with prophetic authority to heal, deliver, and restore in Jesus' name. I recently received this prophetic word concerning God's work among us today:

"What you are viewing is but a preview. I have begun to move around the world and in all the nations, but this is only a preview of that which I shall accomplish. For My Spirit shall begin to flow in unknown and different places. My Spirit shall begin to flow in areas and places where curses have been spoken; but because of My people, blessings shall now begin to be spoken. And My Spirit will be able to find a riverbed to be able to flow through.

"And signs, wonders, and miracles shall glorify My name. Signs, wonders, and miracles shall begin to fall. Yes, signs, wonders, and miracles shall begin to be displayed, for I shall display My glory. I shall take the treasures out of My Kingdom, and I shall begin to lay them upon My beloved. And it shall be a beautiful thing. It shall be a beautiful thing, and you shall see victory where you have had defeat over and over and over. You shall see victory. You shall see victory. You shall see victory!

"Be comforted, be encouraged today. Be comforted and encouraged. You shall eat the fat of the land."

None of this will help us—the sword of the Lord in our mouths, the fire of God in our hearts, the vision of God in our eyes—unless we hear His voice and carefully direct our prayers and deeds where He guides us. We can only tap the full anointing and glory of God when we align ourselves totally with His plan and purpose for the moment.

For centuries, leaders in the Church have studied the Book while discarding the Spirit within the Book (and I love the Word of God as much as anyone). They have intellectually appointed their own priorities and methodologies. As a result, we have reaped a whirlwind of flesh and foolishness in the Church.

We must always approach God in prayer with the biblical premise "...that He is, and that He is a rewarder of those who diligently seek Him" (Heb. 11:6). Prayer is, and always shall be, a *supernatural* act. It is communion with the God of the universe who is Spirit, not flesh. The sword of the Lord is sharpest and most effective when wielded by the Spirit of God through yielded vessels. This is the heart of prophetic intercession and a prophetic people.

Endnotes

1. Source: "Pacific Northwest Prophecy Page" (http://www.kalama.com/~debodino), Dave Bodin, editor. Based in Kelso, Washington, this Internet site presented the unabridged prophecy given January 20, 1997, at the third anniversary [of the Father's Blessing] meeting of Toronto Airport Christian Fellowship in Toronto, Ontario, by Carol Arnott.

2. W. Terry Whalin, "Evangelist Ruibal Slain in Colombia," *Charisma* magazine (April, 1996), 16,18.

Chapter 8

"X" Marks the Anointing

I'll never forget the night Steve Penney, a prophet from Australia, called all the young people forward for prayer in Sunderland, England. He had just finished his message on "Generation X" at Ken and Lois Gott's church, and I was part of the multinational ministry team on stage that night. We were ministering in true "tag-team" fashion (or "cross-pollination" mode), and the Presence of God was incredibly powerful as the young people came forward.

The power of God suddenly hit me, and the spirit of intercession came over me with such power that I fell to the floor. Any other time, people might have noticed me trying to crawl or roll to a place where no one could see me, but not that night. I shouldn't have bothered to get out of sight. Then a spirit of weeping came over me and I wept and wept.

Finally, one of the other members of the ministry team asked if I would pray over the young people as a mother and release a spirit of intercession on the young generation. I couldn't speak because I couldn't stop weeping! Finally,

I took the microphone and tried to pray, but I had to give it up because all I could do was weep. I ended up back on the floor again and the waves of heartbreaking sobs and tears just kept coming. Finally I became concerned over the depth of the pain I was feeling in intercession and I said, "Lord, what is this?" He immediately answered, "It is Rachel weeping for her children." I cried so hard that night that I could barely open my eyes the next day.

The Double-Portion Generation

I asked, "Lord, why Rachel? Why not Leah?" I knew the Messianic prophecy of Jeremiah quoted in the Gospels that described King Herod's slaughter of male children. He had tried to kill the baby Jesus, thinking the Messiah would act like a rival king who would take his earthly throne. Matthew cited Jeremiah's ancient warning, "A voice was heard in Ramah, lamentation, weeping, and great mourning, Rachel weeping for her children, refusing to be comforted, because they are no more" (Mt. 2:18). I thought, *Why not Leah? Leah was the mother of the tribes of Judah. Why Rachel?* And all of a sudden it dropped into my spirit: *Leah had many sons, but Rachel had Joseph—the **double-portion son**.*

Then I realized that God was saying that this so-called "Generation X" will be a double-portion generation! They will have a tremendous anointing from God. That helps explain why they are hidden in the world so that even the enemy doesn't know where they are or suspect their divine destiny. Just as God moved on Joseph to take the infant Jesus and His mother, Mary, to be hidden in Egypt until an appointed day of safety, God has hidden a whole generation of young people in obscurity, and even the enemy doesn't know who they are.

The appointed time of return is here. God is issuing a mighty call for this army to rise up from the shadows of anonymity. We will see thousands and thousands of young people being swept into the Kingdom because they are the next generation with a mighty power and their time has come. It is time to possess the land.

Rachel bore a son to Jacob in his old age, and that was Joseph. Joseph was the embodiment of the "X" generation. He was separated from his heritage and his father, and he was left for dead and sent into bondage in Egypt. Jacob, now called Israel, thought he had simply lost his heritage in Joseph forever. When Joseph was restored to him, *a double portion* blessing was delivered that day!

Jacob was so overjoyed to see his long-lost son and his grandsons that he told Joseph the he would consider Joseph's sons to be *his own sons*! Instead of giving Joseph the one share he would normally receive as one of Jacob's 12 sons, Jacob gave a portion to each of Joseph's two sons, along with the sonship rights enjoyed by the other 11 sons. The Bible record speaks of a "tribe of Joseph," but it also speaks of the tribes of Ephraim and Manasseh (see Josh. 16:8; Rev. 7:6,8). Joseph's family line received a double portion.

Something unusual happened when Jacob delivered the patriarchal blessing to his two grandsons. Although Joseph carefully positioned the two boys in front of Jacob with Manesseh, the oldest, closest to Jacob's right hand (the hand of power and authority in ancient and modern Middle Eastern cultures), Jacob surprised everyone. He crossed his right hand over and placed it upon the youngest son, Ephraim, who was to the left; and put his left hand on

Manasseh, the firstborn son. (His arms formed an "X" in the process, and by this parabolic action he was foretelling the destiny of this generation.) Although Joseph instinctively tried to correct his father's error so he would do it "right," Jacob firmly made it clear this was no mistake, and this blessing was no formality.

As he would with each of his sons in succession, old Jacob literally prophesied the future to his grandsons, but neither the prophecies nor his "methodology" conformed to tradition. He said:

> ...*He* [Manasseh—"causing to forget"[1]] *also shall become a people, and he also shall be great; but truly his younger brother* [Ephraim—"double fruit," from a root word, *Ephrath*, another name for Bethlehem![2]] *shall be greater than he, and his descendants shall become a multitude of nations* (Genesis 48:19).

This speaks volumes to the prophetic Church. This foreshadows the relationship between law and grace and the Jonathan/David ministry relationship of John the Baptist and Jesus Christ. It also symbolizes the older Manasseh generation of believers who will "serve" the younger Ephraim generation by equipping, training, and assisting them for the greatest harvest and avalanche of glory this earth has ever seen.

Peter the apostle preached in Jerusalem after the Holy Spirit fell on the 120 in the upper room, quoting from the ancient prophecy of Joel: "And it shall come to pass in the last days, says God, that I will pour out of My Spirit on all flesh; your sons and your daughters shall prophesy, your young men shall see visions, your old men shall dream dreams" (Acts 2:17). Then he demonstrated from the

Scriptures that Joel's prophecy had begun to be fulfilled that day almost 2,000 years ago!

Welcome the "Survivor Generation"

The marketing world has dubbed this generation, "Generation X," claiming its members had no unique identifying characteristics, goals, or roots to anchor their lives. The marketeers are wrong. The previous generation grew up under the constant threat of nuclear annihilation during the Cold War, but "Generation X" is the generation that the enemy has tried to destroy from the womb! It was this generation that somehow survived the mass mayhem created by the Supreme Court's ruling that legalized abortion nationwide. Almost one out of every three unborn children were "legally murdered" by abortionists before they ever emerged into the light of day, effectively making "Generation X" a "survivor generation" from the moment of birth! Both Moses and Jesus knew what it was like to belong to a survivor generation. They understood what it was like to grow up in a world with significantly fewer people "their age" than there should have been. It seems that satan has always targeted generations of "messiahs and deliverers" for early death.

Satan has reason to worry. The so-called "Generation X" has been marked out and reserved for God. This is a generation of deliverers that have been drawn from the waters of adversity just as Moses was before them. We will see them rise up as apostles, prophets, evangelists, pastors, and teachers, uniquely equipped to reach their own. I believe that God will move upon them in incredible intercession, and I can tell you we are already seeing evidence and fruit of it in Brownsville.

We often see that prophetic intercession will indicate major events or themes of the Holy Spirit in the main revival services that follow. On one particular Friday evening, we held our usual water baptism service with testimonies in the revival meeting before going on to the main service. As soon as the water baptism was over, a powerful spirit of intercession began to move through the congregation as they worshiped, and we soon learned that something momentous was taking place among some of the children.

Angie, an assistant to the children's pastor at Brownsville Assembly of God Church, Vann Lane, brought eight young girls into the service who were weeping and wailing for souls in intense intercession that was even more loud than that of the adults! When Evangelist Stephen Hill asked the congregation to quiet while he spoke to them, everyone quickly stopped what they were doing—except for the eight young girls. They weren't being disobedient; the Spirit just refused to stop what He was doing through them. We didn't realize that at the time, so Angie did her best to move them out to a hallway just behind the platform so they wouldn't disturb the service. What happened next was captured on video, and Vann Lane describes it in his book, *Children of Revival*:

> "She managed to get the shaking, weeping little group that far; then they fell under the power of God right there in the little hallway. An usher closed the doors on either end of the corridor to try and contain the wailing. Angie sent someone to get me [Vann Lane] so that I could see what was going on.
>
> "I opened the door to the hall and could not stand because of the presence of the Lord. I knew Pastor

John [Kilpatrick] needed to see this. I went and got him. He, too, could not stand because of the intensity of God's presence. Pastor John went back into the sanctuary and spoke to the people from Matthew 21:13-16 where Jesus said 'My house shall be called the house of prayer,' and 'Out of the mouth of babes and sucklings Thou hast perfected praise.'

"Then Pastor John sent someone with a microphone to the little hallway. The heart-wrenching, anointed intercession of those eight little girls turned the church upside down. I had never before seen the power of repentance as it happened that night.

"With the voices of the children wailing in the background, Steve Hill exhorted the congregation to believe for the salvation of their family members. 'People are being birthed into the Kingdom right now,' he said....

"The spirit of intercession descended on the people. Brother Steve said, 'If you have a problem with this kind of service, you need to look in the Bible. Read about the miracles and the signs and the wonders. Read about the earthquakes and the salvation conversions. Read about a typical day in the early Church.'

"Then Brother Steve said, 'Strongholds were broken tonight.' "[3]

When the altar call was given that night, people flooded the altar. Large trash barrels were brought in because hundreds of people began to throw their "articles of affection" into the trash barrels—including everything from condoms to drug paraphernalia and other personal items representing strongholds of the world in their lives. Since then, the spir-it of intercession has continued to move among these small children week after week.

Young People and Revival Go Together

Zealous young people have figured prominently in most if not all of the major revivals in Church history. The "Jesus people" movement of the late 60's and 70's involved hundreds of thousands of young adults from both drug backgrounds and church backgrounds. Although we remember the mighty move of God on Azusa Street in 1906, the outpouring of the Holy Spirit actually began among some young people praying for "more" in a small Bible school in Topeka, Kansas. This experience was "transported" to Los Angeles by Brother Seymour, and the rest is history. Many moves of God have actually been started or were really ignited by young people.

I was sharing this information with some visitors from England, and they told me about their recent trip to Argentina. They had visited a church in Argentina that is called "The Children's Church." I think they told me that the oldest child there was 16 years old. The children do the preaching and the worship, and many of the children are intercessors. This intercessor friend from England said that service in Argentina was one of the most powerful meetings he had ever attended. He spoke of the time a small child prayed for him and said, "That kid had to get on a chair to pray and prophesy over me. When the power hit me, I landed on the floor! The power of God hit me stronger during that prayer than at any time adults have prayed for me!"

On Friday night, April 10, 1998—just before I made the final changes to this book—the Holy Spirit especially demonstrated to us at the Brownsville Revival that "God is no respecter of persons" (Acts 10:34 KJV). Children's Pastor Vann Lane holds a special daytime session each Friday for any visiting children's pastors or workers. On this particular day, a visiting children's pastor from Gainesville, Georgia, asked Pastor Lane if his children's group could receive prayer from the children of Brownsville to "cross-pollinate" them with God's Presence.

At the conclusion of the altar call in the main service when special prayer is offered, this children's pastor brought the children from his church back to the children's chapel. Vann had forgotten about the appointment for prayer, so he had to find some of his children quickly. When he opened the doors of the two rooms where the children were, he discovered that they were already praying for one another. He quickly found four of his most dedicated "prayer warriors" in the group and brought them into the cafeteria area to pray for the visiting children.

Within moments the floor was strewn with 14 visiting children and their pastor! The word spread out into the halls and adults and teens alike began to request prayer as well. Vann Lane said, "The news of what was happening contin- ued to spread, and adult prayer team members, tired from the night's revival ministry duties, began to flood into the room as well. All who were prayed for by this young team were touched powerfully by God through these little ones. Several adults were knocked to the floor the moment they entered the room!" Cindy Lewis, a long-time member of

Brownsville Assembly of God and a parent of one of the children praying that night, said:

> "This was the most incredible night of my life. You see, our church has been in revival for two years, and it has changed all our lives without measure. But April 10, 1998, is a night I will never forget! It was Friday night, and God was moving all over the campus. It was late [around] 12:00 midnight, and my husband and I were going to get our children from the nursery—or so we thought. On our way we heard people talking about little children praying for adults and how the power of God was falling. Our little girl is 10, and has been gifted with intercession. When my husband and I arrived in the cafeteria, we stood in total awe...[we saw] little children laying hands on adults and teenagers and the *power of God* touching the people! Many were shaking under the power, many were falling to the ground. Many of the people were getting on their knees so that these children could reach their heads to pray for them.

> "Time after time, people lined up before these little ones. The anointing and Presence of God was powerful. Words could not express the sight that lay before our eyes. I stood against the wall with tears running down my face at the awesomeness of God. The little children were like mighty warriors. [I thought,] *This is our little girl...look what God is doing!* There was such an overwhelming joy. What does one say except, 'Thank You, Father. Thank You. Thank You.'

"Then it happened. One of the workers motioned for me to come for prayer. I quickly shook my head no, then I became convicted and jumped to the middle of the floor and Nicole (not my daughter) began to pray for me. It was like [feeling] electricity shooting through my body. The power was incredible. Something hit me in the pit of my stomach. I bowed over, and I hit the floor. Then I felt many little hands on my back, and I heard tiny little voices praying out to God. Moans from deep in the pit of my stomach began to pour forth, and I shook under the power of the Lord. God is raising up a new generation, one that wants their own testimonies. They no longer want to be entertained, they simply want more of the Lord. What more could one ask for?"[4]

Pastor Lane told me, "It all began in a nursery for the six to nine-year-old children of volunteer workers. The worker responsible for their care was teaching on Pentecost (praise God for teachers who teach instead of merely playing games with our children!). She told the children that we are experiencing the power of God weekly in our revival and children's church services, and she said, 'Pentecost is not just for *then*. It is for now, and it is for you.' The children decided to lay hands on one another and pray. Of course, the power of God fell, and that was where it all began."

When a group of 10- and 11-year-old kids asked the younger group to pray for them, the power of God fell on them as well. And it was from this group that Pastor Lane chose his prayer warriors. He said, "One of the children asked me if I wanted prayer too, but I was hesitant to be prayed for because I was responsible for overseeing the room. After a quick scan of the room, I agreed and was soon on the floor with the others. I had been extremely tired prior to this and found over-abundant strength after this time of refreshing from the Lord through the hands of a ten-year-old!"

Craig, the five-year-old son of one of the senior deacons, was prayed for one night and went out under the power for quite some time. When his mother, Susan, retrieved him, he told her that he had seen Jesus and was called to preach and lay hands on the sick. Like so many of "us moms," Susan wasn't too sure about all of this. But the following week, Craig again received prayer and Susan's doubts melted away. This time Craig told her that not only had Jesus appeared to him, but He was accompanied by a boy and a girl. Little Craig's comment was, "The boy looked just like me, and he even said his name was Craig."

What Craig did not know was that his mother and father had lost two children through miscarriage before he was born. This set his mother's mind at ease and gave her great joy to know that the completed family awaits them in Heaven. As you can imagine, I let this little guy pray for me anytime he wants to! His father, Craig Senior, told me they were recently in Norway conducting ministry. He had just finished preaching and was faced with singlehandedly ministering in prayer to about 500 people! He began to pray, and then he saw one of the pastors suddenly fall to the floor to his left, beyond his reach. Little Craig Junior had sized up the situation and decided to help his dad out. He had begun to lay hands on some of the leaders, and they were being mightily hit by the power of God as they lined up to have him pray!

God is up to something, and we need to honor the children and the youth of "Generation X" because they are at the core of what He is doing. I believe one of the reasons God has moved so mightily in Brownsville is that Pastor John Kilpatrick and Stephen Hill very strongly honor the children and the young people. I believe Jesus has something to say about our treatment of children that we need to heed:

At that time the disciples came to Jesus, saying, "Who then is greatest in the kingdom of heaven?" Then Jesus called a little child to Him, set him in the midst of them, and said, "Assuredly, I say to you, unless you are converted and become as little children, you will by no means enter the kingdom of heaven. Therefore whoever humbles himself as this little child is the greatest in the kingdom of heaven. Whoever receives one little child like this in My name receives Me. But whoever causes one of these little ones who believe in Me to sin, it would be better for him if a millstone were hung around his neck, and he were drowned in the depth of the sea" (Matthew 18:1-6).

We quickly realized that many of the souls—especially the young converts—had come to Jesus because our teenagers and children had gone out and brought them in. These young people know where the harvest is.

One teenager in our church named Jill persevered in prayer and persistent "knocking" on the doors and hearts of school authorities until she was allowed to start a Bible club in her middle school. The students in this Bible club don't just meet and talk. Jill preaches the gospel in these meetings.

They reached capacity in the classroom where they were meeting and even met outdoors for a while until they could find a larger classroom.

The Kids Fell to Their Knees

One day Jill was concerned because she didn't have a "message" for the meeting that day, despite her prayer and preparation. In fact, she didn't have anything until the students filled the room and the Presence of God permeated the classroom. They decided to have an altar call right then, and this young lady leaned over to another student from our church and said, "Can you feel that?" They both felt an unusual heat or warmth in their hearts, as if they were about to "explode." In that moment, the kids in the room instantly began to fall to their knees and began to cry and weep in repentance (this was a public school during a voluntary meeting).[5]

I could go on and on, but because this is very personal, I must include this next story. When my oldest son, Bob, and my daughter-in-law, Cindy, moved here from Southern California with my two teenage grandsons, both grandsons were in great rebellion. They felt like they were moving to the end of the world (compare Pensacola with Los Angeles). That was before the Lord got hold of them in the revival. My oldest grandson, Robby, had received prophetic words as a small child that he would be sent to the nations to preach. We have always held these words before God's throne as a promise, and we often reminded Him of His promise.

Nothing could have looked less likely when Robby arrived from California with his family. Now Robby is studying at the Brownsville Revival School of Ministry and is preparing to "go to the nations" exactly as God declared years ago! The transformation is wonderful. Robby stands out in most crowds because he is so tall. On many nights of the revival, I watch him worship God without inhibition on the front row. He looks like a living "pogo stick" as he jumps up and down with the other young people! Now both of my grandsons sing in the youth choir that ministers at every Saturday night revival service. I say, "Thank You, Lord!"[6]

In Numbers 13, the Lord told Moses to send spies into the land of Canaan. When they returned, they all confirmed that Canaan was a "land of milk and honey." But 10 of the 12 spies focused on the "ites" occupying the land instead of on the wealth of the land God had already promised them. Then Caleb stood up and urged the Israelites, "Let us go up at once and take possession, for we are well able to overcome it" (Num. 13:30b). That prompted the ten negative spies to give their report an extra boost and expand their negative descriptions to include the words *all*, *giants*, and *grasshoppers* for maximum effect:

> *...The land through which we have gone as spies is a land that devours its inhabitants, and all the people whom we saw in it are men of great stature. There we saw the giants (the descendants of Anak came from the giants); and we were like grasshoppers in our own sight, and so we were in their sight* (Numbers 13:32-33).

Too many of us in the Church are like the fearful spies. Although they might have been out of Egypt, Egypt was not out of them! There is still some "Egypt" left in us in the form of a "slave mentality" that says that we cannot overcome and that the devil is bigger than the God within us. Like the Israelites, we'd rather grumble and cry or "choose a new leader" than actually risk crossing the Jordan river to take the land.

When Joshua and Caleb told the Israelites not to fear the "ites," the congregation wanted to stone them (see Num. 14:9-10). Nothing is new under the sun. If you begin to say, "We can take the land!" and tell people that God is moving in your nation, expect trouble. If you begin to declare that revival is not only "intended" but is already upon us, somebody will try to throw stones at you. At least you're in good company.

These Are Scary People

Forty years later, Moses and a whole new generation of Israelites again stood on the banks of the river Jordan. Everyone who had been above the age of 20 the first time Israel stood on the banks of the Jordan had died, and God had raised up a new generation to cross the Jordan and claim the promised land. I believe God has brought the Church to a spiritual river Jordan in this day, and once again, a young generation is being raised up. This army of children and young people is a fearless generation that the enemy had intended to use for evil, but God is using them for good. When the world looks at this "Generation X," they say, "Oh, these are scary people; they are going to rule our country." Yes, Lord. Amen.

Once a week I lead an intercessory prayer meeting for the students at the Brownsville Revival School of Ministry. At the conclusion of one of these meetings, a precious young man named Nahum, who is attending the school from a Third World country on scholarship, approached me in tears. He said that he wanted to publicly confess and make himself accountable to the student prayer group for failing God. Now, every pastor and teacher knows this kind of thing can touch off a touchy situation simply because you never anticipate what a young person might say! But I felt it was appropriate nevertheless. Nahum stood before the group and began to tearfully relate what had happened to him the Sunday before.

> "It was time for the offering, and when I asked the Lord what I should give, He spoke to me to give everything in my pocket. I was concerned because *all* of the money I had was *in my pocket*—$120. I began to bargain with the Lord: "Maybe we could split the money…." But each time I heard "ALL." Finally, I asked the Lord if I could give Him $100 dollars and keep $20. This was met with silence from Him, but when the offering plate reached me I placed $100 in the plate and kept $20.

> "At the conclusion of the service, someone came up to me and placed something in my pocket. After leaving the building, I looked in my pocket and pulled out $100! The Lord said, 'Here is your money back. I asked you for *everything.*'"

Needless to say, my eyes were no longer dry as I searched my own heart and compared the amount of dedication displayed by young people like Nahum against my own. Society has left this new generation in a "gray" zone without any absolutes or instruction about how to direct and live their lives. "Nothing is really all that bad," they are told, "as long as you're not hurting anyone else. After all, your emotions and drives are natural. Just let us help you regulate them." But this generation is not content with platitudes. They are searching for truth. And when they are touched by God's power and taught godly goals of overcoming and holiness as a basis for changing their world, they go for it!

This redeemed "Generation X" is indeed frightening to the complacent Church. They make us face our lack of total commitment. The actions and dedication of these young warriors should bring us to our knees in heart-searching repentance. Every member of "the older generation" (including myself) must heed this wake-up call and let the walls that divide us come down. We must accept, encourage, and lead the new generation into divine possibilities.

God has purposely raised up "Generation X" for "such a time as this" (see Esther 4:14). Just as the young generation was led across the Jordan and into conquest by some faithful members of the older generation of Israel, so will the faithful leaders of my generation lead the armies of young people across our modern river Jordan. Those believers who have seen the miracles and continued to believe God for the fulfillment of His promises will be like Joshua and Caleb. They will help to lead the mighty armies of young people into the promises of God and the harvest.

Those of us who have been touched by revival in the past still have it burning in our hearts for the most part. When I say "touched by revival," I am obviously referring to being touched by the unchanging God, and that is something you never forget. If you've ever been touched by revival, then you were changed forever. It was back in the early 60's that

I was touched by God's Presence in revival, and my whole life was forever changed. Although things got very dull, old, and "religious" for a season, I could never deny the reality of the day I was touched by the power of God. When you have seen God do tremendous miracles, when you have felt His Presence and seen multitudes of souls come to the altar to be saved, delivered, and set free, you won't forget it. You will carry that in your heart forever and constantly pray, "God, You've done it once. Do it again."

That is what my husband and I prayed for, desired, preached, and believed to see for 35 years; and I'm over-joyed to tell you that we are beginning to see it right now across the globe. Make no mistake: *We haven't "arrived" yet.* What we are seeing now is just a tiny beginning of what God wants to do.

The Lord wants to move all over the earth, and He is busy setting His Church free so that its members can get busy with the work of the ministry (see Eph. 4:11-12). He is on the move to bring souls in, but we haven't seen any-thing yet. There is a harvest, and there is a Canaan land for us to enter and begin to claim the promises. What do you suppose the new generation of Israelites saw once they crossed the river Jordan into Canaan? In many cases, they found that the inhabitants had fled in fear before them, leav-ing behind crops that were already planted, and vineyards ready for harvest. There were homes left for them that were fully furnished and ready for them to possess. This is also a picture of what is waiting for the Church. The harvest is already out there. The grapes are ripe for the picking. The land of milk and honey is ready for us, but it will take the trusting obedience of believers who are willing to trust God and believe in His promises to take the land for Christ.

This Is One Inheritance You Can Have Now!

We all know that Joshua and Caleb were two "old timers" who were allowed by God to cross the river Jordan with the young generation because of their good report the first time around. But many people don't realize that Eleazar the priest was also allowed to cross the river as one of the priests who helped carry the ark of the Presence across the river Jordan (see Num. 34:17). Now, those priests were not part of the spies selected from among the 12 tribes of Israel. The priests were not considered a tribe of Israel in this respect; they were not given an inheritance because God Himself was their inheritance. As a nation of intercessors, priests, and kings, we are like the Levites—God is our inheritance. We have been given the great privilege of bearing the ark upon our shoulders as we prepare to cross our modern river Jordan in the flooded waters of *harvesttime* (see Josh. 3:15).

I believe that Psalm 102 is a timely word for "Generation X" believers today. It declares:

> *This will be written **for the generation to come**, that a people yet to be created may praise the Lord. For He looked down from the height of His sanctuary; from heaven the Lord viewed the earth, to hear the groaning of the prisoner, to release those appointed to death, to declare the name of the Lord in Zion, and His praise in Jerusalem* (Psalm 102:18-21).

I believe that our "Generation X" is God's marked generation of deliverers for this day. They are the *generation to come.* The river of harvesttime is rising, and it is time for God's people to ford the river of faith into His land of promise.

Endnotes

1. James Strong, *Strong's Exhaustive Concordance of the Bible* (Peabody, Massachusetts: Hendrickson Publishers, n.d.), **Manasseh** (Hebrew, #4519).

2. Strong's, **Ephraim** (Hebrew, #669, 672, 6509).

3. Vann Lane, *Children of Revival: Letting the Little Ones Lead* (Shippensburg, Pennsylvania: Revival Press, 1998), 47-50. If you would like to hear more about this service and God's mighty work in and through the children at Brownsville Assembly of God, I highly recommend Vann Lane's life-changing book. A videotape of that service, entitled "Lord Have Mercy II," is also available through Brownsville Assembly of God Church, 3100 West DeSoto Street, Pensacola, Florida, 32505; (904) 433-3078.

4. Cindy Lewis, as told to the author.

5. Jill's testimony appears in Brownsville Youth Pastor Richard Crisco's book, *It's Time: Passing Revival to the Next Generation* (Shippensburg, Pennsylvania: Revival Press, 1997), 122-124.

6. Robby was also interviewed in Richard Crisco's book, *It's Time: Passing Revival to the Next Generation*, on page 124.

Chapter 9

The Spirit of Jezebel

And Ahab told Jezebel all that Elijah had done, also how he had executed all the prophets with the sword. Then Jezebel sent a messenger to Elijah, saying, "So let the gods do to me, and more also, if I do not make your life as the life of one of them by tomorrow about this time." And when he saw that, he arose and ran for his life... (1 Kings 19:1-3).

In the timeless realm of the spirit, the same malevolent spirit of rebellion that motivated King Ahab's Phoenician wife, Jezebel, to slaughter God's prophets and threaten Elijah still roams the earth and launches schemes to destroy God's leaders today! As we draw closer to the return of Christ and the anointing of Elijah is released, we need to be alert... "lest Satan should take advantage of us; *for we are not ignorant of his devices*" (2 Cor. 2:11).

No book about intercession or a mighty move of God would be complete without addressing the ancient spiritual enemy of true prophetic leadership and ministry and the strategy that God wants us to use against "the spirit of Jezebel." Don't fall into the trap of thinking, *Oh, Jezebel was a mythological Old Testament character. She's dead now, so Jezebel has nothing to do with* **real life** *today. She's just an old symbol of wanton, seductive women.*

Look to the Scriptures. Wherever the glory of God alights on the lives of His people, the darkness of satan's fury and jealousy will tag along, hoping to stop, hinder, or taint God's leaders. The Jezebel spirit "followed" the prophetic anointing of Elijah all the way into Jesus' day to murder John the Baptist (the greatest of all the prophets), and it showed up in the end-time Book of Revelation! The prophet Malachi set the stage when he prophesied:

> *Behold,* ***I will send you Elijah the prophet before the coming of the great and dreadful day of the Lord.*** *And he will turn the hearts of the fathers to the chil-dren, and the hearts of the children to their fathers, lest I come and strike the earth with a curse* (Malachi 4:5-6).

This is the last prophetic word given in the Old Testament canon, and it spoke of the coming of the spirit and declarative prophetic anointing of Elijah. Another ancient "anointing," if you will, passed through time as well—the satanic spirit of Jezebel, which was rooted in the child-sacrifice cult of Baal and Ashtoreth (a mythological "husband-wife" team of demons). In my opinion, there is considerable evidence that the "Jezebel" spirit is really the demonic principality of Ashtoreth (Astarte in Moab, Ashtar or Ishtar in Babylon and Assyria, and Aphrodite-Venus in Greece and Rome) operating through or upon human beings. Almost every ancient Middle Eastern nation called this murderous spirit "the queen of heaven." It should really be called the demon of murder, lust, jealous control, and cruel domination.

The best way to understand the nature of this ancient demon spirit's attack on God's leaders is to examine its schemes and methods in the original confrontation between Elijah the prophet and Jezebel. The conflict began when Ahab launched his 22-year reign over Israel by marrying Jezebel, the daughter of the king of Sidon, and by importing her god (Baal) and goddess (Ashtoreth) as the new national deities. God immediately sent His prophet, Elijah, into Ahab's capital in Samaria with a prophecy that neither rain nor dew would fall on the land until Elijah said so (see 1 Kings 17:1). This was especially embarrassing since Baal was a Canaanite "rain god"!

While Elijah was restoring the life of a widow's son in Jezebel's homeland of Sidon (see 1 Kings 17:7-22), Jezebel was busy killing all but 100 prophets of God in Israel in an attempt to wipe out all traces of the true God from ancient Israel. After three years had passed, God told Elijah to confront King Ahab, and then He would bring rain (see 1 Kings 18:1-4).

Elijah challenged Ahab to bring his 450 prophets of Baal and Jezebel's 400 prophets of Ashtoreth to Mount Carmel for one of the most incredible showdowns in history. These "prophets" weren't just your everyday variety of idolaters— they were intimate associates of Jezebel, her personal charges and friends and perhaps paramours. The Bible says they literally "ate at her table." They were dedicated to the service of Baal, the "weather god," and of Ashtoreth, supposedly the goddess of fertility, the womb, war, and love.

The real truth is that when archaeologists excavated the ruins of a temple of Ashtoreth at Megiddo near Samaria, they also unearthed a cemetery just a few steps away that contained many jars holding the remains of infants sacrificed to Ashtoreth in the temple. In other "high places," archaeologists discovered the remains of infants and small children in the temples themselves and buried in the walls of buildings as "foundation sacrifices." These child sacrifices were coupled with orgies using female and homosexual prostitutes in honor of Ashtoreth. In the words of H.H. Halley, "Prophets of Baal and Ashtoreth were official murderers of little children."[1]

You probably already know what happened. Elijah challenged the prophets of Baal to call on their "god" to consume their sacrifice with fire from heaven. When nothing had happened after half a day of frenzied prayer, begging, and dancing, Elijah began to mock the false prophets and their unresponsive idols of wood and stone. In desperation, the prophets of Baal turned to their tried-and-true techniques of bloody self-mutilation, and they prophesied until the day was nearly over while the people of Israel watched and yawned, but Baal was neither listening nor talking that day (see 1 Kings 18:29).

The people of Israel had agreed to Elijah's challenge that "...the God who answers by fire, He is God" (1 Kings 18:24b), and it was God's turn. Elijah called the people of Israel over to watch him rebuild the altar of God, stack the wood, and place the sacrificial bull on the pyre. Then he dug a ditch around the altar and offered a final indignity to the crowd of idolatrous Baal worshipers; Elijah confidently challenged the people to flood the altar, the sacrifice, and the wood with four water pots filled with water. If this was going up in flames, then he would make it even more of a miracle for Jehovah God. Elijah told them to soak it a second time, and then a third. Finally, he completely filled the ditch around the altar with water and prayed a short and simple prayer.

God answered by sending such an intensely hot fire from heaven that it consumed the sacrifice, the wood, and even the stones of the altar! Almost as if God wanted to finish off the meal with some water, the flames even "licked up" the water in the ditch (see 1 Kings 18:38). Elijah immediately ordered the astounded Israelites to seize the prophets of Baal and Ashtoreth, and then he killed all 850 of them at the brook Kishon (see 1 Kings 18:40). Immediately afterward, Elijah prayed and released the rains of God (the life-giving rains of God always seem to come after the cleansing fires of God). What happened after that is a prophetic parable that fully reveals the schemes and techniques of the Jezebel spirit. We need to be especially alert after a great victory over the enemy.

The Technique of Intimidation

The Bible tells us that Elijah sent word to King Ahab to get into his chariot (Israel was known for her extensive collection of horses and chariots) and to rush back home before the supernatural rain cut off his route home to Jezreel, Ahab's capital city at the entrance to Megiddo (or what was later called Armageddon in Revelation 16:16). Then the Spirit of God came upon Elijah, and he literally outran King Ahab's war chariot and his fastest horses to the front gate of Jezreel and waited for him there as if to seal the defeat of Israel's idolatrous king. The trouble started when Ahab did what he also did years later at the end of his reign—he "ran to momma," or in this case, *Jezebel.*

> ***And Ahab told Jezebel*** *all that Elijah had done, also how he had executed all the prophets with the sword. Then Jezebel sent a messenger to Elijah, saying, "So let the gods do to me, and more also, if I do not make your life as the life of one of them by tomorrow about this time." And when he saw that,* ***he arose and ran for his life...*** (1 Kings 19:1-3).

What Is Wrong With This Picture?

Isn't this the same prophet of God who declared a three-year drought and then prayed and saw a deluge of rain fall on the land? Isn't this the prophet who called down fire from heaven to embarrass satan's representatives right in front of the people of Israel in the most dramatic spiritual confrontation of the Old Testament? Isn't this the man who single-handedly killed 850 prophets of Baal and Ashtoreth with his own sword that same day? Isn't this the man who then pulled up his robes and supernaturally outran King Ahab's fastest war chariot over a 20-mile distance *to intercept Ahab* at the gate to his own stronghold in Jezreel? (Elijah should have been exhausted after the test by fire and the task of personally executing 850 demonic prophets with a sword.)

Why would this mighty prophet work an unbroken string of miracles all day, only to run away in fear over the secondhand threats of Jezebel that evening? (Elijah was so frightened that he fled for almost 100 miles until he reached Beersheba, which was outside of Israel's borders in the territory of Judah.)

The problem wasn't Jezebel; it was the *evil spirit* behind Jezebel that this prophet feared. Although Elijah may not have realized it (we don't know at this point), he had been intimidated by the threats of a demonic principality or fallen angel, and his reaction was similar to the way most people react to the presence of a holy angel—with fear. Although Ahab, as king of Israel, had entire armies at his command, he felt powerless against the prophet Elijah. Jezebel had no armies, but the demonic principality operating through her was quick to strike out with threats of death against God's leader. (This evil spirit was of a higher order than those operating in and through the prophets of Baal.) I believe it was God's perfect will for Elijah to hold his ground and deal with Jezebel and the spirit right then and there; but Elijah didn't stay to pray or seek God's face. He simply ran for his life.

The Technique of Isolation

It wasn't until Elijah was alone on Mount Horeb, more than 195 miles from Beersheba and almost 300 miles from Jezreel, that he was able to hear God's still small voice and receive specific direction. Yet God asked him a question two separate times on the mountain that clearly indicates Elijah was in the *wrong place doing the wrong thing!* Twice God asked, "What are you doing here, Elijah?" (see 1 Kings 19:9,13) The first time that God asked this question, He received the whiny answer of a man who had been isolated from his destiny by fear, shame, and self-pity:

So [Elijah] *said, "I have been very zealous for the Lord God of hosts; for the children of Israel have forsaken Your covenant, torn down Your altars, and killed Your prophets with the sword.* **I alone am left;** *and they seek to take my life"* (1 Kings 19:10).

God told the prophet to "Go out, and stand on the mountain before the Lord" (1 Kings 19:11a). After God demonstrated His total power over wind, earth, and fire, He spoke softly to Elijah, and in verse 13, we are told that Elijah "...wrapped his face in his mantle and *went out and stood* in the entrance of the cave" (1 Kings 19:13a). In other words, Elijah had again moved from his assigned spot because of fear. He was hiding inside the cave instead of standing outside on the mountain. God asked him for the second time, "What are you doing here, Elijah?"

God intended for His prophet to be standing at the gate of Jezreel, the seat of satan's stronghold over Israel. Instead, Elijah was a defeated man who even felt he had to hide his face from God. The Lord was gracious and merciful, and He instructed Elijah to anoint Hazael king over Syria, Jehu king over Israel (in Ahab's place), and Elisha as prophet in his own place (see 1 Kings 19:15-17). Between the three of them, these men would accomplish what God originally wanted to accomplish through Elijah alone. But God still used Elijah to drive the final prophetic nail home in Ahab and Jezebel's spiritual coffin to end Elijah's prophetic mission on a high note.

The Technique of Manipulation and Domination

Evil or not, God still worked through King Ahab in the meanwhile to protect the remnant of 7,000 faithful followers in His beloved Israel. When God delivered King Ben-Hadad and all Syria's armies into King Ahab's hands, Ahab arbitrarily decided to spare the king and restore his lands even though God wanted him destroyed. As a result, God sent another prophet (not Elijah this time) to prophesy his death. Ahab went home in a bad mood, and he decided that he needed to take his neighbor's vineyard (the man's family inheritance) to make himself feel better. When the neighbor, Naboth, refused to sell or trade with Ahab, he went to bed and sulked like a little child. He even refused to eat. When Jezebel found him pouting, he told her his sorry story, and she said, "I will give you the vineyard of Naboth the Jezreelite" (1 Kings 21:7b).

Jezebel's actions reveal the same techniques used today by the ruling spirit that possessed her. She boldly used the authority and name of another (Ahab) to set up the wrongful accusation and death of an innocent man—all to please her husband and to secure an even stronger hold on the throne. She hired two men to falsely accuse innocent Naboth and steal his vineyard...does this sound familiar? The scribes and Pharisees hired false witnesses to falsely accuse Jesus before the Sanhedrin, hoping to steal away His inheritance, the "vineyard" of Israel. Countless numbers of pastors and church leaders can tell you painful stories of this exact scenario played out in detail until they were driven out of their churches and their reputations and ministries assassinated by false witnesses and behind-the-scenes schemes of others. The spirit of Jezebel is a master of manipulation, particularly where unspiritual individuals, groups, or institutions are concerned. Another trademark is that most of the time, the Jezebel spirit will recruit other people to do the actual dirty work of slander, judgment, and outright attack. Only the Spirit of God can bring its hidden darkness out into the light for all to see.

The Baby With a Time Bomb

A few years before joining Brownsville, I had a prophetic dream. My husband and I were associate pastors at another church at that time, and I knew enough about intercession to pay attention to my dreams and pray over them, although I didn't understand the power of intercession to the extent I do now. This dream was heavy with symbolism, and I did not comprehend what it meant at the time.

I saw a toddler standing on the front steps of a tall building, and many of our congregation members were milling around in the same area. When I approached the child out of curiosity, I saw that it had a crude time bomb attached to its back, and the timer had a very short time left before the device would detonate. I began running around trying to get someone to call the bomb squad, but no one seemed to be concerned—even after I pointed to the bomb. When it became apparent that we would not have time to disarm the bomb, I quickly caught up the child in my arms and ran away from the area as fast as I could so the explosion would not harm other people.

When I felt I had gone far enough away from the others, I put the baby down with the intent of running to safety myself. But I found that I could not leave the child alone! I threw my body over the child in this dream, and it reminded me of soldiers who would fall on booby traps to save their fellow soldiers. I was praying and hoping for a miracle, committing myself and the baby into God's hands. Suddenly the bomb went off and I awoke. I knew that I had received a warning about an impending danger to our church and I immediately went into prayer, but I certainly had no idea how the danger would come or from what direction. For several months I periodically prayed and presented this dream to the Lord, but I did not receive any further understanding.

I was not familiar with the tactics of the "Jezebel spirit" at the time, but about one year before I received this dream, someone joined our church whose ambitions, methods, and operation perfectly matched the classic profile of the "Jezebel spirit." Immediately, this individual began to woo the leadership (including my husband and I) with flattery, gifts, and constant offers ("I'm *always* ready to help..."). My husband and I both felt "red flags" go up in our spirits, so we maintained a polite distance from this individual. We watched as this person systematically wove a web around members of the senior pastor's family. Eventually this individual gained a position of authority in the church by always being around the leaders.

In due time, the person's sensual tactics of seduction began to become very apparent. I am thankful to say that the senior pastor was not affected, nor were any of the other leaders. But when the pastor found it necessary to remove this individual from a position of leadership, the person's true intent was exposed. Our pastor was lied about and his character was maligned by this individual, who made open overtures to other people in an attempt to get corroborating accusations (the Bible calls them "false witnesses"). We were privately apprised of the situation by our leader who assured us that the accusations were untrue.

Finally, this individual phoned to tell me something that this person brazenly said would "...blow this whole church up!" (These were the person's exact words.) As you can imagine, when this person used that particular terminology, my mind immediately went back to my prophetic dream, and everything fell into place. The innocent child was our pastor, and this malicious attack against him was a plot to destroy him and our church! The Lord had used this dream to give me a supernatural prayer assignment to cover him, and I was to protect him to the death. However, the Lord had disarmed the "bomb" with intercession. Much to the chagrin of this individual, this devious attack didn't negatively affect our pastor, nor did it harm our church, all praise be to God!

Jezebel's Great Weakness

One of the great weaknesses of the Jezebel spirit, as well as those under its influence or control, is that there is an unavoidable tendency to forget about God and His habit of intervening in the affairs of nations and the Church. Just when the forces of evil think that it's safe to foreclose on stolen property, goods, or people, God shows up! Hallelujah!

In Ahab's case, it was Elijah again. And this time, Elijah didn't hold back. He didn't stop until he had accurately foretold the violent deaths of judgments over Ahab, Jezebel, and every single one of their descendants, relatives, and friends. The final statement about Ahab sheds a bright light on the most significant technique used by the spirit of Jezebel: "But there was no one like Ahab who sold himself to do wickedness in the sight of the Lord, because Jezebel his wife *stirred him up*" (1 Kings 21:25). The Hebrew word for "stirred" is *cuwth*, and it means "to prick, stimulate; by implication to seduce:—entice, move, persuade, provoke, remove, set on, stir up, take away."[2] The spirit of Jezebel is a manipulating and dominating spirit that will stop at nothing to hinder

God's people and replace light with darkness. Ahab found this out the hard way.

The Technique of Entrapment by Betrayal

In that same year, during Ahab's twenty-second year as king of Israel, God engineered Ahab's downfall and allowed what I believe was the Jezebel spirit to play the part of seducer, traitor, and betrayer. This is the fate that ultimately comes to individuals *used* or influenced by Jezebel spirits for evil purposes. (There is no "loyalty" among the ranks of darkness.) A man named Micaiah confronted some false prophets telling Ahab to go into battle with this blunt warning:

> *And the Lord said, "Who will persuade Ahab to go up, that he may fall at Ramoth Gilead?" So one spoke in this manner, and another spoke in that manner. Then a spirit came forward and stood before the Lord, and said, "I will persuade him." The Lord said to him, "In what way?" So he said, "I will go out and be a lying spirit in the mouth of all his prophets." And the Lord said, "You shall persuade him, and also prevail. Go out and do so." Therefore look! The Lord has put a lying spirit in the mouth of all these prophets of yours, and the Lord has declared disaster against you* (1 Kings 22:20-23).

Ahab ordered that the prophet be thrown in prison, and followed the advice of the false prophets. He was killed that day in complete fulfillment of Elijah's prophecy. At this point, Elijah's three successors took front stage and began to systematically kill every member of Ahab's family and following. But true to the end, Jezebel was determined to try her last and perhaps most desperate technique to preserve her unholy hold on power and authority in Israel and escape the sword of Jehu, the newly crowned king of Israel.

The Technique of Seduction

Jehu was a former royal bodyguard and a hardened soldier with little, if any, mercy. He was a perfect choice for the job of destroying Ahab's family and descendants. He had a very clear understanding of the root of Jezebel's power. He told her son, Joram, just before he killed him, "What peace, as long as *the harlotries of your mother Jezebel and her witchcraft* are so many?" (2 Kings 9:22b) When Jehu finally tracked down Jezebel, her final technique was revealed: "Now when Jehu had come to Jezreel, Jezebel heard of it; and *she put paint on her eyes* and *adorned her head*, and looked [leaned seductively] through a window" (2 Kings 9:30).[3] If the spirit of Jezebel cannot intimidate a man or woman of God, it will try to isolate him or her. If that fails, it will try to manipulate and then dominate him or her (the use of betrayal for entrapment is usually used on people who have been used for evil purposes by the spirit of Jezebel). The most well-known (and least expected) technique of the enemy is to use sexual seduction to woo God's servants into sin and ultimate destruction. In Jehu's case, his eyes were wide open. He had seen for himself just how ruthless and dangerous Jezebel was, and he wasn't fooled by her makeup, her dressed hair, or her flattering looks from her bedroom window. Jezebel was thrown out of her window by two eunuchs (who were also impervious to her sexual advances) and was trampled to death by horses.

Every year, we hear of Christian leaders of both genders falling into adultery and other sexual sins—even though in many cases there was no pattern of previous sexual sin or deep-seated problems. Further investigation will often prove that these people have fallen into a carefully crafted demonic scheme of seduction. I've heard it said that the enemy has a "woman" or a "man" for every major leader, and this person is directed like a walking time-bomb into their church offices, health clubs, and counseling rooms at exactly the wrong times and seasons. As intercessors with a prophetic mandate, we need to be like Jehu—anointed, forewarned through discernment, and forearmed as warriors, impervious to the charms of the Jezebel spirit and the people used by it.

The Jezebel Technique of Impartation

One of the worst characteristics of the Jezebel spirit is its ability to impart or move from one person to another, like bacteria or a virus. When King Jehoshaphat of Judah allowed his son, Jehoram, to marry King Ahab's daughter, Athaliah, he didn't know it, but he was importing the spirit of Jezebel into his household and bringing about his own destruction as well. Athaliah was just as bad or even worse than her mother! The familiar/familial spirit of Jezebel seems to gain more power and influence as it is passed down from generation to generation. After King Ahab's death, Jehu went after Ahab's sons and also killed his son-in-law, King Jehoram as well (Athaliah's husband).

Athaliah's reaction was incredible. She immediately began to systematically murder every possible heir to the throne except herself, which specifically included her own sons and grandsons! What kind of woman was this? This is the mark of demonic activity because such cold-blooded murder of your own family isn't natural. Only one grandson, Joash, the sole remaining heir in the royal line of King

David, survived Athaliah's rampage. He was hidden away by his aunt, and he later became one of Judah's greatest and most godly kings. My point here is that the "spirit of Jezebel" is a spirit, not a person. It moves easily from willing person to willing person, and from age to age, because it is, after all, a spirit.

The Jezebel spirit is a murderous spirit with a commission from satan to destroy the seed of the righteous. It is this same Jezebel spirit that is driving the abortion movement and infiltrating the feminist movement in our day! Had Athaliah succeeded in her attempts to destroy all her sons and grandsons, then the last earthly remnant of David's seed would have been killed, which would have meant no Messiah in the lineage of David could have come to the earth. All God's prophetic declarations through the prophets were dependent on the survival of one little boy. Yet God had made David a promise, and He sovereignly moved upon people and world events to preserve David's seed. We serve that same covenant-keeping God today, and He is still moving to preserve the seed of the righteous.

The Jezebel Spirit and John the Baptist

*Assuredly, I say to you, **among those born of women there has not risen one greater than John the Baptist**; but he who is least in the kingdom of heaven is greater than he. And from the days of John the Baptist until now the kingdom of heaven suffers violence, and the violent take it by force. For all the prophets and the law prophesied until John. **And if you are willing to receive it, he is Elijah who is to come*** (Matthew 11:11-14).

Jesus made it clear that the same spirit that was upon Elijah was also upon John the Baptist. Yet even this powerful prophet had to contend with the likes of Jezebel. What happened when the same foul spirit of Jezebel rose up against him? *John lost his head!* This ancient spirit had totally engulfed the life of Herodias, the wife of Herod Antipas, who was holding John in his prison at the time. Herodias' life and actions paint a perfect picture of the spirit of Jezebel at work.

Herodias was the *daughter* of Herod Antipas' half-brother, Aristobulus. She had been married to another half-brother of Antipas named Herod Philip I before she married Antipas. According to the late Dr. Merrill C. Tenney:

> "When Antipas went to Rome he stayed with Herod Philip who was living there as a private citizen, and became enamored of Herodias. Antipas promptly divorced his own wife, who was a daughter of the Arabian king Aretas. Aretas' daughter, learning of Antipas' intentions, fled to her father, who made war on Herod...Herod carried through with his marriage with Herodias, who, with her daughter Salome, joined him at Tiberias."[4]

The spirit operating in Herodias was a master manipulator with a lust for power and a hatred of the truth. Evidently, Herodias' first husband didn't have enough power and wealth for her, so she ruthlessly snagged someone else who had what she wanted. She orchestrated the breakup of two marriages to create a new incestuous bond, and she quickly began to manipulate and dominate Herod Antipas. She became the real power behind the throne. (Her lust for power led to Antipas' downfall later on when she pressed him to demand a royal title from the infamous Roman Emperor Caligula and Antipas was deposed.)

Salome was Herod's step-daughter, and when she danced for him on his birthday, that dance wasn't a waltz or a cute little ditty done before a loving father. It was a sensuously seductive dance that ignited the fires of lust in Herod to the point where he literally promised Salome anything she wanted up to *half of his kingdom* (see Mk. 6:22)!

Salome was so controlled by the Jezebel spirit in her mother that she asked Herodias what to ask for, and she was promptly told to ask for the head of John the Baptist (although this wouldn't benefit Salome in the least). In the words of Dr. Tenney, "Although Herod seems to have respected the blunt honesty of the prophet who rebuked him boldly for his misdeeds, Herodias was infuriated and finally succeeded in securing his death. Antipas was too weak or indifferent to justice to save the life of the man who had told him the truth."[5] The Jezebel spirit will always move to cut off authority, using whatever means necessary.

If You Take a Stand, Expect Jezebel to Show Up

If you take a bold stand for the Lord in your church, city, or nation, you can be certain that at one time or another you will encounter the spirit of Jezebel. This spirit shows up (as if under assignment) wherever God's Spirit has begun to cleanse a people and restore the glory of God to its proper place. I feel this was one of the dangers the Lord had in mind when He spoke to Pastor Kilpatrick about "guarding" the revival through increased intercessory prayer. If you are a pastor or church leader, you have probably already felt or dealt with the presence of a Jezebel spirit in your church or ministry at some time in your life. (Note: The Jezebel spirit is neither male nor female; it is a spirit without gender. It simply takes on feminine characteristics or operates through female human beings more often to approach and neutralize predominantly male church leaders.)

Wherever God's Spirit is working, especially when you begin to have revival, the spirit of Jezebel will rise up to try to hinder and drive you out before your time. When I go to a certain state, I often feel this driving spirit to run and get away. I remember a time when I conducted a meeting there and returned home sensing a heaviness that lasted three days. I thought, *Lord, what is this?* I couldn't function, let alone teach. I felt depressed, tired, and driven. I wanted to quit ministering and just walk away and disappear! I was in the middle of a wonderful revival, and I was having the time of my life in the Presence of God night after night. So what was it? I paced the floor all that day and went back and forth from worship to praise, but it felt "dead," like the heavens were brass. I prayed, "Dear God, what is this? I can't go on unless You show me what this is."

I spent much of the night on my face before God in prayer, and finally I went to bed. In the middle of the night I felt a pressure on my chest and heard the words, "The spirit of Jezebel." I said out loud, "Of course. It's the driving spirit of Jezebel, the one that is always trying to drive you out." From that point on I knew what I was dealing with. If that spirit is ever allowed to infiltrate a local church and exert control, it will try to remove or discredit leadership and drive out everything that is godly and holy, to replace it with Baal. Sexual immorality will begin to surface, along with strife and disunity. In varying degrees, that spirit rules over geographical areas and influences the actions of the people there—including many Christians—with hopelessness, discouragement, and fear.

Jesus spoke to John the apostle with unusual harshness concerning the spirit of Jezebel operating through a woman in the church at Thyatira. That ancient spirit is clearly active in the world today, and the Lord wants us to root out that spirit and deal with it, or else we will be held accountable for our own folly.

> *I know your works, love, service, faith, and your patience; and as for your works, the last are more than the first. Nevertheless I have a few things against you, because you allow that woman Jezebel, who calls herself a prophetess, to teach and seduce My servants to commit sexual immorality and eat things sacrificed to idols. And I gave her time to repent of her sexual immorality, and she did not repent. Indeed I will cast her into a sickbed, and those who commit adultery with her into great tribulation, unless they repent of their deeds. I will kill her children with death, and all the churches shall know that I am He who searches the minds and hearts* (Revelation 2:19-23a).

The Watchmen on the Wall and the Fall of Jezebel

This spirit was totally mastered and defeated in the Old Testament passages describing the downfall of Jezebel's daughter, Athaliah. What was really defeated here was the spirit of Jezebel, the evil principality that despises God's glory and His leaders. A confrontation took place when the time came for the one surviving grandson of Athaliah and descendant of David to rise up and take back the throne that was rightly his. It meant a face-to-face confrontation with the spirit of Jezebel in Queen Athaliah (who had seized all power in Judah for six years). A priest named Jehoiada, the husband of the woman who hid Joash from Athaliah, made a united front by organizing loyal captains, guards, and Levites after showing them Joash, God's hidden revelation (see 2 Kings 11:4-16). The Levites protected the young child until the time of revealing. Intercessors are to function in that same way, protecting in prayer the purposes of God until the appointed time.

The priest assigned a third of them to watch the king and his house (God's anointed leader and his family), a third watched the house of God (the priestly duty of watching God's people), and a third watched the door of God's house and the altar (as gatekeepers and protectors of God's Presence, His holiness, and His purposes in the earth). As intercessors, God's people are His watchmen on the wall and gatekeepers. God doesn't need protection, but we do. He has armed us with powerful weapons and unfailing "spiritual intelligence information" for a reason: *We are to be the watchmen on the wall.* Intercession is prophetic; it "goes ahead." God will reveal to us in prophetic intercession every plan and plot of the enemy so He will be glorified through our obedience and victory. Leaders would do well to occasionally lend an ear to their trusted intercessors. It is my firm belief that in order to fully disarm the authority and power of Jezebel in churches, it will be necessary for the pastoral staff, worship team, and the intercessors to walk in unity and mutual trust, allowing their diversity of giftings to work together.

When Jehoiada and his sons anointed young Joash as king of Judah, they clapped their hands and made a great noise (see 2 Kings 11:12). When we lift up Jesus Christ the King in our midst, God is well pleased, and His glory begins to descend on His people. That tends to flush out the spirit of Jezebel from its hiding places in the hearts of mis-led men and women. When Athaliah heard the noise of the people clapping and praising God and their new king, she boldly ran right into the house of God and saw King Joash standing by the entrance. He was surrounded by an impen-etrable bodyguard of leaders, trumpeters, singers, and war-riors who were rejoicing, blowing trumpets, and being led in praise to God by the singers.

Athaliah foolishly tore her clothes and shouted, "Treason, treason!" (In her demonic delusion, she still thought that *she was the authority* and that God's chosen leader was the usurper—some things never change.) What caused her to expose herself and come out? It was the praise and the worship! Athaliah was immediately removed from God's house and executed, which effectively destroyed the earthly vehicle used by the spirit of Jezebel. Satan and his servant the spirit of Jezebel despise anointed music that glo-rifies God. They hate joy, and above all, they hate and fear the glory of God. The spirit of Jezebel cannot prosper where God is lifted up in anointed worship, praise, and unity.

There is no reason for a man or woman of God to fall under the influence or attack of the ancient Jezebel spirit today!

How can I say such a thing? We have the Blood of the Lamb of God to wipe away every sin and remove every hold of satan on our lives. We have the indwelling Spirit of the living God in our hearts to guide and teach us in all things. We have the written Word of God, and we have the opportunity to tap the power of the Body of Christ unified in intercessory prayer. We have that formidable list of weapons described by Paul the apostle in Second Corinthians 10 and Ephesians 6. Best of all, we have the Presence of God Himself! All these work together to support and protect God's leaders, God's people, and God's purposes in the earth today. All we need is knowledge, wisdom, and the will to act in obedience to the Spirit of God. This is the purpose of prophetic intercession, and it can be summed up in the simple statement of Scripture: "For as many as are *led by the Spirit* of God, these are sons of God" (Rom. 8:14).

Endnotes

1.   Henry H. Halley, *Halley's Bible Handbook* (Grand Rapids, Michigan: Zondervan Publishing House, 1973), 198-199, see also 166-167, 206. This source cites the archaeological findings of the Oriental Institute of the University of Chicago, the Palestine Exploration Fund, and others.

2.   James Strong, *Strong's Exhaustive Concordance of the Bible* (Peabody, Massachusetts: Hendrickson Publishers, n.d.), **stirred** (Hebrew, #5496).

3.   According to *Halley's Bible Handbook*, archaeologists with Harvard University, Hebrew University of Jerusalem, British School of Archaeology, and the Palestine Exploration Fund found "in the ruins of Ahab's 'ivory house' saucers, small stone boxes, in which Jezebel mixed her cosmetics...they still had traces of red." See *Halley's Bible Handbook*, 206.

4. Merrill C. Tenney, *New Testament Survey* (Grand Rapids, Michigan: Wm. B. Eerdmans Publishing Co., 1961), 37.

5. Tenney, *Survey*, 37-38.

Chapter 10

Crossing the Jordan

"It was daylight when I went in. I remember that I first knelt by the side of the empty Tomb [of Jesus in Jerusalem] and prayed, then I lay down in the empty Tomb and read the scripture of Galatians, where Paul speaks, 'Yet not I, but Christ liveth in me. The life I now live in the flesh I live by the faith of the Son of God who loved me and gave Himself for me' (Gal. 2:20).

"Once again time had lost its meaning, I was lost in prayer. This time God was to do a new thing for me, something I had never known before of His love and compassion. Suddenly the empty tomb became filled with light. I did not realize it was a light from another world, I only knew that I could feel His power and presence. I must have shouted very loudly, because suddenly someone was knocking on the door, asking me if I was all right. I do not know how long I sat after that, but when I came out it was dark—many hours had passed by—but I left something in the Tomb that will never be mine; I took something from it. For God had done a new thing for me that evening in the old Garden Tomb that will never leave me."[1]

Tommy Hicks wrote these words describing his life-changing experience in the tomb of our Lord in Jerusalem in May of 1955, just before he conducted the first evangelistic campaign ever permitted in Communist Russia following World War II, and perhaps since the Bolshevik Revolution of November 1917. God prepared him in the tomb for a "crossing of the Jordan" that would bear monumental fruit in the dark decades to follow. It was during his Russian campaign that Tommy experienced what he considered to be the greatest miracle of his ministry, although God had healed hundreds of thousands of people through his ministry.

Tommy Hicks preached behind the Iron Curtain for 28 days, often speaking up to five times a day. Yet he did it without Christian interpreters in all but two cities. The miracle happened one time when his Russian interpreter suddenly stopped, for reasons unknown to him, and refused to go on. Then she stepped back and spit in his face just before she walked off the platform!

After he wiped his face, Tommy turned to the crowd and began to weep because he had been so deeply hurt. "Suddenly a mighty anointing came upon me, and for several minutes, I spoke with the greatest force I had ever known in all my life, words that I had never learned, nor did I understand. *I was speaking in their language.* Then I turned and asked how many would receive Christ. These words I understood, and to my amazement, more than half of the congregation raised their hands."[2]

We Face Our Own River Jordan

God is bringing the Church to its own river Jordan in this hour. If we take courage and step into the waters by faith, I believe we will experience the manifestation of signs and wonders of all kinds in the midst of the greatest world harvest of souls this planet has ever known! This was confirmed by Dr. Oral Roberts in a prophecy he gave after I'd ministered at a conference for the Foursquare Women International. I will reproduce his message in its entirety because it relates directly to the move of God today and in the days ahead:

> "The Lord spoke to me prophetically through Lila tonight. It was worth my trip just to be with you, but it was doubly worth it to hear this, and Beverly [Bradford, director for the Foursquare Women International] asked me if I had a prophetic word, and I do have a short one.
>
> "Last June the Spirit of the Lord came upon me and said, '*I have seen that healing has been in a slight decline. It has been very strong, it went into a slight decline. I'm going to bring it back big time—big time—big time.*' The word I leave with you is *healing is coming again—Big Time.*
>
> "I tell you another word the Lord spoke to me. I didn't plan to say it, [because] it's not going to be very popular. *We preachers have preached the people to death, but we've not healed them unto life.* The Lord spoke those words to me about a week ago. 'You preachers

are preaching the people to death, but you're not healing them to life.' And I said, 'Lord, You don't want preaching? The Word says that faith comes by hearing and hearing by the Word.' 'Well,' He said, *'I must have preaching, I must have teaching, but I can't leave out the healing power for that is the confirmation that makes the preaching and the teaching stick in men's hearts.'* So that's the word. Does anyone want me to stretch my hand out to you? Is there anyone here who has cancer?"[3]

Every great enterprise that God gives you has a river Jordan to be crossed, land to be claimed, and giants waiting to challenge you! Moses and the children of Israel faced the Jordan twice. Jesus actually inaugurated His ministry with a public baptism in the muddy Jordan. Dr. Edward Miller faced his Jordan as he struggled in lonely prayer for months, only to see victory when the shy bride of a preacher-on-the-run reluctantly agreed to strike a small table in Argentina. Tommy Hicks faced a Jordan when he reached out for the hand of Argentina's dictator, President Juan Peron, and asked God for a miracle. Tommy crossed the Jordan again when he stepped onto Russian soil and faced hostile officials at every turn.

Oral Roberts faced a Jordan early in the 1960's when he looked across a vacant field in south Tulsa and "saw" a university that would raise up young men and women to take God's light and healing power "into every man's world." He dared to cross that Jordan and in 1965, Oral Roberts University received its first students and celebrated its grand opening with Evangelist Billy Graham as the keynote speaker. (After much of the writing for this book was done,

Dr. Roberts confirmed to me that he was teaching his students about the concept of "cross-pollination" in the late 1970's and encouraging them to exchange information, training, and anointing in their various fields of study, ministry, and giftings.)

Randy Clark faced a Jordan when he agreed to preach at a small Vineyard fellowship in Toronto, Ontario. Pastor John Kilpatrick, Evangelist Stephen Hill, and the congregation at Brownsville Assembly of God faced a Jordan when God first descended on them with the weight of His glory on Father's Day of 1995. Their Jordan was found in the questions: Would they go on? Were they willing to have their lives forever turned upside down?

We Haven't Gone This Way Before

God is visiting His people with His glory, and it is now clear that there is a cost that comes with His glory! Will we accept the challenge and wade the river into His greater will? Will we lay down our peacetime priorities and take up the tools of harvest and spiritual warfare? We, like Joshua before us, have come to understand that God's promise of harvest will only come through sacrifice and conquest.

Then Joshua rose early in the morning; and they set out from Acacia Grove and came to the Jordan, he and all the children of Israel, and lodged there before they crossed over. ... and [the officers] *commanded the people, saying, "When you see the ark of the covenant of the Lord your God, and the priests, the Levites, bearing it, then you shall set out from your place and go after it...that you may know the way by*

*which you must go, **for you have not passed this way
before***" (Joshua 3:1,3-4).

God is moving us to new places in Him, and we have
never passed this way before. The principle we see again
and again in God's Word is this: *When you see the Presence
of God in Christ moving, follow Him.* Don't expect God to
follow you! This is never more true than in prophetic intercession and the harvest. The living Ark of the Covenant,
Christ Jesus, is moving, and God's mercy is being poured
out. The Church is being renewed and revived and souls are
being saved as never before in history. That is where God is
going. Are you willing to step into the river and follow
Him? Jesus Christ is being lifted up and He is drawing all
men and nations to Himself on a scale that can never be
accomplished through the mere works of men and women.

For too long we have lifted up our local churches and
our church denominations. We have lifted up our doctrines
and our religion. We've learned the hard way that those
things won't draw anyone anywhere except far away from
God and the Church. They repel the hurting and the lost
because they don't see any light or glory in them. All that
the world has seen for centuries is unending division, bickering, and fighting in the Church, and most of it has been
rooted in what? Endless strife over doctrine and religion.
There is a place for doctrine, but it isn't in first place. That
place is reserved exclusively for the living Lord, the risen
King of kings who has chosen to deal with each of us *personally*, heart to heart, concerning the issues of life. If doctrine was the solution, then the Pharisees were right. They
had countless volumes of doctrine and teachings about doctrine. What they lacked was the living Messiah who walked

among them, seeking a relationship with real people in real life situations. The Bible says, "...the letter kills, but the Spirit gives life" (2 Cor. 3:6b).

People have told me, "I've got enough problems of my own, why would I want to go to church?" I want to tell you that God is bringing unity to the Body of Christ today by calling us all to *sit at His feet* as Mary did (see Lk. 10:39-42). If we ever obey, we will unleash a flood of God's glory, for unity is stronger than division, love is stronger than hate, and light is stronger than darkness.

Foretold by Prophets New and Old

God is rapidly lighting fires of reform, renewal, and revival around the globe, and it has all been carefully orchestrated by the Spirit for "such a time as this." How can I say such a thing? Much or all of it has been prophesied in advance by the prophets. We've already examined portions of the prophecy God gave Tommy Hicks in 1961. We've looked at the prophecy God recently gave us through Oral Roberts concerning what will soon come to pass (through signs and wonders). God's outpouring of love and healing over Toronto Airport Christian Fellowship had been accurately and independently prophesied by many people in many locations over a period of years—including Paul Cain, Marc Dupont, and a Polish-Argentine student named Alexander who didn't even know how to spell or pronounce the city's name in June of 1951!

God's outpouring of glory in Pensacola was accurately prophesied in 1991 by Dr. David Yonggi Cho, pastor of the world's largest church in Seoul, South Korea, while he was conducting a meeting in Seattle, Washington. Pastor Cho prayed, "God, are You going to send revival to America, or is she destined for judgment?" The Lord told him to get a map of America and to point his finger at it, and when he did, his finger was drawn to the city of Pensacola in the Florida panhandle. Then the Lord said, "I am going to send revival to the seaside city of Pensacola, and it will spread like a fire until all of America has been consumed by it." Dr. Cho confirmed the prophecy to a Church of God pastor in Mobile, Alabama, saying, "No rumor! No rumor! Received vision; revival will come!"

Dr. John Hurston, a former associate and spiritual mentor of Dr. Cho, has personally attested to Dr. Cho's vision and prophecy. And Loren Triplett, foreign missions director for the Assemblies of God, described the Pensacola revival at the Assemblies of God national convention in St. Louis on August 12, 1995, and also related this vision and prophecy. Dr. Cho was in the audience at the time.[4]

I've already mentioned a prophet named Dale Van Steenis, who saw a vision of honey dripping from the eaves of the main sanctuary at Brownsville Assembly of God Church even before it had been fully built. There is more. In November of 1989, Michael Ratliff prophesied about a move of God over Pensacola, Florida. The prophecy was delivered in Phoenix, Arizona, after Brother Ratliff had asked his audience, "Is there anyone here who is willing or has been thinking about going to Pensacola, Florida?" A man named Jim Wies raised his hand, and he received this prophecy "in proxy" for Pensacola:

> "Transformation will come. Many people in peril, in dire straits, will be saved dramatically. Healings will take place. Deliverances will take place. And one

church in particular will humble its heart and receive Me. The college people, the students, the high schools, various people will be reckoned with the angels of God that are loosed.

"This is a victory against all contempt that is stirring in the city, actually disarming the time bomb that is ticking away in Pensacola, Florida. You shall see the turnaround and nationally will the Church hear about the revival that sparked in Pensacola.

"And all the enemies of the Lord will be fleeing and screaming and crying out trying to hinder the great blessing of God. And many upheavals will be heard in Pensacola. It will even be publicized. God is preparing and bringing capacity for the righteousness to rise up as a spearhead, many will follow, the whole shaft will go into the heart of the enemy of that city. It will be taken for the Kingdom of God.

"This thing is going to happen in the 1990's not only in Pensacola, but in other cities as well, to shake, and to bring people into ordinance with the Lord for His revival, for His desire to shake the unbelief and to shake the foundations, the traditions away from the people of God."[5]

When the priests of God dare to step into the river Jordan by faith, bearing with them the ark of the Lord, He will rest in the waters with them. Even the crossing will be miraculous. What makes a God-ordained, God-commanded conquest interesting is that the land of promise is always claimed in *the rest of the Lord* rather than the labor of man. This is what Dr. Edward Miller discovered when he decided to veer from "the established methods of missionaries" to seek God's face instead. It is God who builds the house, not man (see Ps. 127:1). We have our part, but only as "people under authority" who "do what we see the Father doing" instead of doing what we merely think is right (see Mt. 7:29; Jn. 5:19). It is time to step out into the waters of our Jordan.

> *Now therefore, take for yourselves twelve men from the tribes of Israel, one man from every tribe. And it shall come to pass, as soon as the soles of the feet of the priests who bear the ark of the Lord,* **the Lord of all the earth, shall rest in the waters of the Jordan,** *that the waters of the Jordan shall be cut off, the waters that come down from upstream, and they shall stand as a heap* (Joshua 3:12-13).

God is moving in intercession today as never before. He is pouring out a passion for prophetic intercession upon the Church and He is doing it for a divine reason. It is time for a great harvest, and the Church must be ready. People around the world who have never experienced the kind of intercession Paul describes in Romans 8:22-27 are beginning to experience it, and it seems like a whole brand-new thing. The truth is that it isn't new; it just seems new to us. Do we manufacture this kind of "outrageous" prayer ourselves? Absolutely not. It comes through the Holy Ghost, and it is directed and initiated by the high priest of our faith, Jesus Christ, the supreme intercessor.

We have "never been this way before" in the sense of the size of the challenge before us, but we have faced challenges, and we have seen glimpses of glory, of prophetic intercession, of prophetic worship, and of supernatural harvests. In a very real sense, we are seeing the "new" being brought out of the "old." In 1993, Jim and Michal Ann Goll led an intercessory prayer mission of 19 intercessors to the site of the original Moravian prayer watch tower in Herrnhut, on the northern border of the Czech Republic. It was there in the eighteenth century that God poured out a spirit of intercession that inspired a 24-hour-a-day prayer watch that continued unbroken for more than 100 years! In his book, *The Lost Art of Intercession*, Brother Goll describes their mission to go to a place where God's image still lingered to ask for the same spirit of intercession God gave the Moravians hundreds of years ago.[6] Their prayer was granted in a supernatural visitation in that tower, and prophetic insight was given that is still coming to pass today!

Agabus the prophet "acted out" his prophecy about Paul's future imprisonment in Rome by tying himself up with Paul's belt while delivering his prophecy (see Acts 21:10-11). As early as 1918, Aimee Semple McPherson was tapping into the power of prophetic intercession to conduct spiritual warfare when violent threats and attempts at physical intimidation were made by organized gangs of angry men during the "Nation-Wide Camp" meetings in Philadelphia. Mrs. McPherson dismissed the first meeting early and called for an all-night prayer meeting to pray for those who had been disrupting the meetings, and many stayed to pray. After about two hours of fervent prayer, according to an eyewitness report quoted by Church historian Richard Riss in his book, *A Survey of Twentieth-Century Revival Movements in North America*:

"When the praying had ceased, Sister McPherson, in that simple way of hers, said:

" 'Now, dear ones, just let us be quiet and see what God has for us' ...Sister McPherson had retired to one end of the rostrum, where she swayed back and forth in a peculiar step or dance. This continued for some time, when suddenly she moved rapidly to the great upright piano, and began to play in the Spirit. The moment the first strange chord was struck, all eyes were riveted upon her. Wonderful music flowed from the keys as her hands flew rapidly to and fro....

"She then arose and gave a message in tongues, using certain things to emphasize her words. She took a megaphone which stood near at hand, and filled it with flowers from a vase on the pulpit, which typified the 'horn of plenty.' Next, placing the flowers on the floor, she watered them from a pitcher, showing that His saints would be revived and watered with the Latter Rain, which would soon fall upon them, and then closed with an exhortation to get ready for the soon oncoming of King Jesus."[7]

After that night of prayer, the agitators seemed to disappear. In Aimee Semple McPherson's words, "The opposition has melted away like snow before the sunshine."[8] As happens so often when a battle is waged through worship and praise and prophetic intercession, the Spirit of the Lord seemed to join in the victory celebration!

"As the holy anthem broke forth, Sister McPherson seemed to float toward the piano, with uplifted hands and transfigured face, and commenced to play and sing in the Spirit. We had heard spiritual songs before, but never like this...we were transported with ecstasy, and we were in the Spirit and were singing the New Song without any effort on our part.

"Oh, the precious, heavenly music! Who can in any way describe it? We could only compare it to an aeolian harp with its rising and falling cadence, and its sweet, blended harmonies, only far sweeter and more pure in tone than the finest pipe organ, for this was the Holy Ghost playing upon God's great instrument not made with hands."[9]

This expanded prophetic expression is what we call prophetic intercession. It is an unhindered yielding to the Holy Spirit to pray the heart and will of God into the earth as it already is in Heaven. An early healing evangelist, Maria B. Woodworth-Etter, often stepped into prophetic intercession or saw those in her meetings begin to physically "prophesy" to the people during her crusades. One church elder wrote of one of her meetings in San Diego:

"There were marked demonstrations of the Spirit on the lines of messges in tongues and interpretations; also some very remarkable manifestations through the saints, as they were used of God to bring forth the scriptures which apply definitely to these last days.

"One of these I will mention briefly. The power of God came upon one of the sisters in the back part of the hall. She came quickly to the front, taking off her hat, coat and other loose articles of apparel as she went. (Stripping for the race. Heb. 12:1.)

"Turning the pages of her Bible as she went rapidly. (He who runneth may read. Hab. 2:2.)

"Going forth along the altar up to the gates (the narrow way), to a closed door at the farthest corner of the long hall. There she knocked on the door and continued knocking harder and harder, but no response. Then after a time the truth seemed to dawn upon her mind—that she was shut out...

"Soon another saint was led under the power over the same route, hopping along, up to the door. She knocked and continued knocking harder and harder. Getting down upon her knees, begging and entreating and wailing, but the 'door was shut.'

"Such wailing as she retraced her steps, going all the way back on her knees.

"The presence and power of God was so manifest at these clear demonstrations in the Spirit of just what is going to take place so soon in the lives of many professors. A holy awe filled the hall and sinners were convicted and saints made to humble themselves anew before God. Amen."[10]

Prophetic intercession can only be done using all of our being, according to the great commandment—with all our heart, soul, strength, and mind (see Mt. 22:37). We are the Body of Christ upon the earth, and so we, the Church, are supposed to share in His intercessory ministry. As our Head intercedes, so should we become intercessors for the world.

The Elders and the Young Warriors Cross Together

Another key parallel between the Joshua and the Israelites and the Church today is the relationship between the older generation of leaders and the younger generation of believers who are being swept into the Kingdom. Once again, God is placing elder priests and intercessors, the priests, prophets, and warriors who spied out the land a generation and more beforehand, at the head of a younger army of young men and women with a prophetic mandate to take the land. There is no room for bickering or "sharing God's glory." It all belongs to Him and to Him alone.

Just as in Joshua's day, God is exchanging the old manna, the bread of survival in desert seasons, with the honey of promise. When the Israelites refused to believe God and chose the desert over the promised land, God allowed that generation to fully reap what they had sown. Everyone over the age of 20 lived and tramped around that desert until they died (see Num. 14:29)! And God supernaturally sustained them with provisions, but the manna He gave them also contained a painful reminder of "what might have been" (see Ex. 16:31). Manna contained the "taste" of honey, a continual hint of what could have been their holy inheritance by faith. The younger generation under Joshua's command had grown up in the desert eating manna since their weaning. Once they crossed the Jordan, the manna ceased to come and they began to live off the fruit of the promised land. For the *first time in their lives*, this new generation of faith began to taste the "real thing," the honey of the hive. They could never again be content with just a "taste" once they had enjoyed the real thing!

We have been "sustained" and have survived on "tastes" of what could and would be some day. But the taste of honey—of God's glory—was always just a brief hint, a flavor, mixed in and almost lost among the common elements of our existence. As we now cross the Jordan into an unprecedented season of harvest, the manna of yesteryear has suddenly stopped. God urges us to cross the river and "taste and see that the Lord is good" (see Ps. 34:8). He welcomes us to feast with Him at His feet. The days of second-hand news and watered-down honey flavoring are over. He wants us all—every one of us—to taste His glory and be transformed! We are not going to be spoonfed by the Lord anymore. This is not a new thing—it was prophesied and foretold by the prophets long ago.

> *Simon has declared how God at the first visited the Gentiles to take out of them a people for His name. And with this the words of the prophets agree, just as it is written: "After this I will return and **will rebuild the tabernacle of David**, which has fallen down; I will rebuild its ruins, and I will set it up; so that the rest of mankind may seek the Lord, even all the Gentiles who are called by My name..."* (Acts 15:14-17).

God was declaring through the prophets that He will rebuild the tabernacle of David. Now David's primary ministry was as *a warrior* and *a prophetic worshiper*. He was one whom the Lord used to prophesy on the harp. Demons would flee when he played and worshiped. The psalms form the basis for most of our songs and hymns to this day. Psalm 149 provides the premiere description of "warfare by praise" as it declares:

> *Let the **high praises of God** be in their mouth, and **a two-edged sword in their hand**, to execute vengeance on the nations, and punishments on the peoples; to bind their kings with chains, and their nobles with fetters of iron; to execute on them the*

written judgment—this honor have all His saints. Praise the Lord! (Psalm 149:6-9)

God makes it clear that there is a direct correlation between worship and warfare. The enemy will always come in and attempt to thwart the worship in a local community of faith *because God still sets worshipers in front in time of war.* I've noticed over and over again in 35 years of ministry and pastoral work that the greatest conflict in the local church usually erupts in the worship department. The enemy works overtime to plant pride among worship leaders and musicians. Why are we so surprised, if it is true, as some Bible commentaries assert, that the prophetic Scriptures about the King of Tyre have a dual interpretation and refer to lucifer/satan as the former praise and worship leader of Heaven?

*Thus says the Lord God: "You were the seal of perfection, full of wisdom and perfect in beauty. You were in Eden, the garden of God...**The workmanship of your timbrels and pipes was prepared for you on the day you were created.** You were the anointed cherub who covers; I established you; you were on the holy mountain of God; you walked back and forth in the midst of fiery stones. You were perfect in your ways from the day you were created, till iniquity was found in you"* (Ezekiel 28:12b-15).

I believe that lucifer was indeed the praise and worship leader in Heaven before he fell because of pride (see Is. 14:12-17). Unfortunately, this is a natural inclination for those with beautiful and very visible giftings. I have no negative feelings about people who are involved in leading praise and worship; quite to the contrary, I highly esteem those anointed psalmists who are able to lead God's people into the throne room. These are simply areas where we need to be constantly vigilant in our lives.

The spirit of control will always be a particularly dangerous possibility in this area. Why? Worship and praise is one of the most powerful vehicles for warfare in the realm of the spirit because it is *eternal*. When we leave this world, we will take nothing with us except the souls we won to Christ and our worship and praise! Worship and praise is eternal. It was in existence before the earth began. It is the highest form of warfare to defeat the devil while honoring God. When we exalt God and His Son in praise and worship, we literally begin to occupy satan's previous place of power and control. No wonder he fights our worship and praise to God so strongly!

Worship and Our War With Darkness

I asked the Lord for a confirmation or explanation of the role worship plays in spiritual warfare and the battle for lost souls. Somehow I was beginning to believe that praise and worship was intimately linked with spiritual warfare, but I wanted some extra confirmation. Then I took a flight home from Michigan and overheard a young man in front of me give his testimony to a flight attendant. (I couldn't help but hear the conversation—if you have flown economy class, then you know what it is like to be a "captive audience" to any nearby conversation.)

This young man told the attendant, "When I hit the floor, I was instantly saved and delivered." Now that statement caught my attention, although it was obvious that the flight attendant wanted to be anywhere else than stuck on that airliner listening to that man witness to her. I saw the man again at the baggage claim area and I said, "I couldn't help but hear your conversation with the flight attendant. May I ask you what you are doing here in Pensacola?" He said, "There is a revival going on here, and I've heard that it is awesome. I haven't been there yet, though. This is my first visit to the revival, but people are getting saved, and I know God is really going to touch me." (I found out later on that he was an acquaintance of Lindell Cooley, the worship leader at Brownsville.)

I just had to dig a little deeper. "I heard you say that you were knocked to the floor at your conversion...." He nodded and said, "It was something else. I was at home, and was trying to figure out how I was going to get enough drugs to get me through the evening. I wasn't thinking about God. In fact, God wasn't in my vocabulary, nor in my thoughts. For the longest time, I hadn't had any interest in Him. God was far away from me, but as I reached for the phone I was violently thrown to the floor. And when I came up, I was saved, delivered from drugs, and my whole life was changed!"

Nobody was in the room with him, and no, he wasn't even close to the city of Pensacola when it happened! He said for about two weeks he went around saying, "Oh God, you must have some wonderful love for your good servant." He felt like God had stopped all Heaven just to zap him because he was "special." But then the Lord said, "*It had absolutely nothing to do with you*. There was a woman who was constantly worshiping and praising Me, and she got into My throne room. I was *so pleased and so filled with her worship* that I asked her, 'What do you want?' *She said, 'I want Wayne' and I* [God] *said, 'You've got him.'* "

I received a second confirmation one day when a young lady came up to me during a teaching session at the Brownsville Revival School of Ministry and said she was from another state. She and a couple of other intercessors had attended a meeting where I had taught about prophetic intercession, and the husband of one of the ladies had been violently opposed to her coming, which had resulted in a big conflict. She didn't know what she was going to face when she got home. On the long trip home, this woman expressed her concern about a confrontation with her husband, and the woman who told me this story said, "Do you know what we need to do? Let's just see if that stuff Lila teaches works." So they decided to praise and worship God all the way home, and they kept calling out this man's name as well.

That woman's husband was actually visiting the School of Ministry the week this young woman told me this story, and he confirmed it with this testimony. He said, "I was just minding my own business at work and the Holy Ghost came on me. The power of God arrested me and instantly changed my whole attitude!"

If you read about the great moves of God in the past as I have, if you investigate the journals and biographies of those involved in the great revivals in this century and before, you will notice that in every case, public praise and worship to God were prominent, virtually continuous, and very often spontaneous! The worship at the meetings at Azusa Street was legendary for its intensity, and the same can be said for Aimee Semple McPherson's meetings and those of Maria B. Woodworth-Etter, Dr. Edward Miller, and Ruth Helflin as well. The worship would often last far into the night and sometimes into the following day, and there were many reports of "heavenly voices" joining the human voices lifted in praise, with the result sounding like "pipe organs" or other instruments that weren't present at the meetings. This phenomenon was common in the early Pentecostal movement in the twentieth century and in the Latter Rain movement of 1948.

The city of Sunderland, England, has been called by some "the Pensacola of England," because of the powerful outpouring of God's Spirit and Presence there through the ministry of Ken and Lois Gott. They describe experiences of angelic worship that are very similar to those we've just described above, and they first appeared in intercessory prayer meetings conducted by Lois Gott:

> "One memorable evening some six months after we began the prayer meetings, everyone was involved in praying passionately for abused, neglected and hurting children, when suddenly we were silenced by a deafening roar of voices. Most of us fearfully thought that there was a large football crowd gathered outside the building, but the roar of voices was soon followed by drums, cymbals and musical instruments.

> "As we began to enter into worship we were aware of thousands of voices joining in and enveloping us in their melody. In awe and amazement we all stopped to listen, and our elder, Jim Elliott, down-to-earth as usual, stepped forward to see what could possibly be happening. It was obvious that no one in the room was singing and yet there was a multitude of voices worshipping in the Spirit in glorious harmony. It was the most beautiful singing we had ever heard, incredibly

high and with many harmonies. At that point a wind began to blow through the building. We could find no draughts or any other human explanation for it...Some reports of the 1907 revival [in which Smith Wigglesworth was baptized in the Holy Spirit in Sunderland] witness similar angelic singing, while more outlandish meetings are also on record."[11]

This has even happened at Brownsville Assembly of God! In one of his first revival services as worship leader, Lindell Cooley describes in his book, *A Touch of Glory*, the time a staff minister asked him after the service how he cued "the tape" so accurately so that all the voices and instruments matched. Lindell told him there *were no singers* or instruments other than his keyboard, but then Lindell also remembered hearing a beautiful counter melody while leading the chorus. He discounted it at the time because he thought one of his lead singers had just grabbed a free microphone to sing counter melody.

Two men at the sound board remembered hearing the beautiful voices and instruments too because they double-checked the sound board to make sure nothing was turned on that shouldn't have been. Every microphone had been turned off except Lindell's. The extra voices had been supplied from Heaven. As is often the case, Lindell confirmed later that the angelic voices had joined the worship for two reasons: to praise God and to bring deliverance to a young woman suffering from demonic possession who was in the audience that night. As soon as Lindell (and the angel) stopped singing, the woman gave a blood-curdling scream and was instantly delivered from years of torment![12] This is a beautiful picture of spiritual warfare waged through praise and worship. When you begin to hear the heavenly hosts singing in your midst, you can be sure that God is doing something again. It is an indication of His glory in your midst, and whenever spontaneous worship begins to break out, I can guarantee you there is going to be great opposition to it.

The purpose of prophetic intercession and praise and worship is the same. We want Him. We want God to commune with us in all His glory and beauty. We long for His Presence within and without. When we seek His face instead of His hand, He delights to give us *both*! Where His Presence is welcomed, longed for, and sought from the heart, His outward or *manifest* Presence is very often experienced as well.

When God-hungry people empty themselves and hunger and thirst for Him who is our righteousness, His glory will inevitably come to fill their hearts with His Presence. The result is life-changing. When His glory arrives on the scene, you don't have to lay hands on people and pray to see them healed; they will just be healed. Their bodies have no other choice in the Presence of perfection. When His glory enters a building or gathering place, the bound are instantly set free. The captors have no choice in the Presence of all authority and power. The Prince of Peace is in command in that place. There is no room for argument or hesitation. *That's what we want.* We want Him. We want His glory.

My anthem as an intercessor is Psalm 68. This short psalm revolutionized my prayer life and my spiritual battle tactics. I still put on all my spiritual armor, and I still keep it bright and my sword sharp. I want to be instant in season and out of season, when my Lord gives a command. *However*, and this is a very big and crucial however, I don't win battles with my armor and sword. *God wins the battles. I just follow orders.* Look at God's battle plan for conquest and victory in the earth:

> *Let God arise, let His enemies be scattered; let those also who hate Him flee before Him. As smoke is driven away, so drive them away; as wax melts before the fire, so let the wicked perish at the presence of God. But let the righteous be glad; let them rejoice before God; yes, let them rejoice exceedingly. ... But God will wound the head of His enemies... They have seen Your procession, O God, the procession of my God, my King, into the sanctuary. The singers went before, the players on instruments followed after; among them were the maidens playing timbrels. Bless God in the congregations, the Lord, from the fountain of Israel* (Psalm 68:1-3,21,24-26).

The key to the great harvest in this day is "cross-pollination," or unity. God-birthed unity is the true miracle that births prophetic intercession, revival, and the harvest. God purposely designed His earthly body as a whole comprised of many different and totally interdependent parts. He refuses to give any single "part" all the revelation or abilities on any given subject or area. Why? Because that forces us to cross over our artificial lines of division and draw nourishment and insight from our brothers and sisters.

As we begin to lift up the crucified and resurrected Christ and Messiah, He—and He alone—will draw all men unto Him. As intercessors begin to lay their personal agendas aside and begin to minister to the King of Glory, the King will begin to share His heart with them so that they can share in His intercessory ministry. Their prayer will begin to manifest a "divine focus" and sharpness that pierces even the thickest darkness of the enemy. In the words of Tommy Hicks, another knee-worn prayer warrior, *"Where prayer is focused, power falls."*[13]

As the Body of Christ begins to worship God in spirit and in truth (see Jn. 4:23) and realizes that God's house is to be a "house of prayer for all nations," as Jesus declared in Mark 11:17, then the harvest of the millennium will begin in earnest! The battle is the Lord's! Let God arise and His enemies be scattered. Salvation isn't enough. Renewal isn't enough. Revival isn't enough. As the Greeks told Philip in John 12:21, "We wish to see Jesus!"

Arise in our midst, O God.

Endnotes

1. Tommy Hicks, *Capturing the Nations in the Name of the Lord: The Miracle Revival of Russia* (Los Angeles: Manifest Deliverance and Worldwide Evangelism, Inc., n.d.), 10-11.

2. Hicks, *Capturing the Nations*, 25.

3. Reproduced from transcripts of audiotapes of the International Foursquare Church conference, which were graciously provided by Grace Chapel Foursquare Church.

4. These facts have been published by Brownsville Assembly of God in numerous printed materials and on their official website on the Internet at http://www.brownsville-revival.org.

5. This prophetic word was delivered to Jim Wies on behalf of the city of Pensacola by Michael Ratliff in Phoenix, Arizona, on November 12, 1989. Pensacola was

already prominent in the abortion battle due to the bombings of three abortion clinics there in 1989. In 1993 and 1994, abortionists were murdered by extremists, launching a tremendous backlash against the Christian community in general.

6.   Jim W. Goll, *The Lost Art of Intercession* (Shippensburg, Pennsylvania: Revival Press, 1997), 1.

7.   Richard Riss, *A Survey of Twentieth-Century Revival Movements in North America* (Peabody, Massachusetts: Hendrickson Publishers, 1988; 2nd printing, 1995), 96-97.

8.   Riss, *A Survey of Twentieth-Century Revival Movements*, 96.

9.   The testimony of George Lloyd, an eyewitness to the prayer meeting in Philadelphia, as recounted by Richard Riss, *A Survey of Twentieth-Century Revival Movements*, 97.

10.   Elder W.F. Harlow, quoted by Maria B. Woodworth-Etter in her book, *Signs and Wonders God Wrought in the Ministry for Forty Years* (Indianapolis, Indiana: by the author, 1916; reprinted by Harrison House, Tulsa, Oklahoma, n.d.), 460-461.

11.   Ken and Lois Gott, *The Sunderland Refreshing* (London: Hodder and Stoughton in association with New Life Publishing, 1996), 66-67. Used by permission.

12.   Lindell Cooley, *A Touch of Glory* (Shippensburg, Pennsylvania: Revival Press, 1997), 126-129.

13.   Tommy Hicks, *It's Closing Time Gentlemen* (Los Angeles: Manifest Deliverance and Worldwide Evangelism, Inc., n.d.), 16.

Appendix

I have reproduced Evangelist Tommy Hicks' end-times vision that he received in 1961 here in its entirety and unedited form. It is a stunning vision that we are seeing come to pass in our day. Brother Hicks was used by God to lead the powerful 1954 Argentina revival in an explosive 62-day mass evangelism and healing campaign that swept three and a half million souls into the Kingdom of God!

Vision of the Body of Christ and the End-Time Ministries[1]

My message begins July 25, about 2:30 in the morning at Winnipeg, Canada. I had hardly fallen asleep when the vision and the revelation that God gave me came before me. The vision came three times, exactly in detail, the morning of July 25, 1961. I was so stirred and so moved by the revelation that this has changed my complete outlook upon the body of Christ, and upon the end-time ministries.

The greatest thing that the church of Jesus Christ has ever been given lies straight ahead. It is so hard to help men and women to realize and understand the thing that God is trying to give his people in the end times.

I received a letter several weeks ago from one of our native evangelists down in Africa, down in Nairobi. This man and his wife were on their way to Tanganyika. They could neither read nor could they write, but we had been supporting them for over two years. As they entered into the territory of Tanganyika, they came across a small village.

The entire village was evacuating because of a plague that had hit the village. He came across natives that were weeping, and he asked them what was wrong.

They told him of their mother and father who had suddenly died, and they had been dead for three days. They had to leave. They were afraid to go in; they were leaving them in the cottage. He turned and asked them where they were. They pointed to the hut and he asked them to go with him, but they refused. They were afraid to go.

The native and his wife went to this little cottage and entered in where the man and woman had been dead for three days. He simply stretched forth his hand in the name of the Lord Jesus Christ, and spoke the man's name and the woman's name and said, "In the name of the Lord Jesus Christ, I command life to come back to your bodies." Instantaneously these two heathen people who had never known Jesus Christ as their Savior sat up and immediately began to praise God. The spirit and the power of God came into the life of those people.

To us that may seem strange and a phenomenon, but that is the beginning of these end-time ministries. God is going to take the do-nothings, the nobodies, the unheard-of, the no-accounts. He is going to take every man and every woman and he is going to give to them this outpouring of the Spirit of God.

In the book of Acts we read that "In the last days," God said, "I will pour out my Spirit upon all flesh." I wonder if we realized what he meant when God said, "I will pour out my Spirit upon all flesh." I do not think I fully realized nor could I understand the fullness of it, and then I read from the book of Joel: "Be glad then, ye children of Zion, and rejoice in the Lord your God: for he hath given you the former rain moderately, and he will cause to come down for you the rain, the former rain, and the latter rain—" (Joel 2:23). It is not only going to be the rain, the former rain and the latter rain, but he is going to give to his people in these last days a double portion of the power of God!

As the vision appeared to me after I was asleep, I suddenly found myself in a great high distance. Where I was, I do not know. But I was looking down upon the earth. Suddenly the whole earth came into my view. Every nation, every kindred, every tongue came before my sight from the east and the west, the north and the south. I recognized every country and many cities that I had been in, and I was almost in fear and trembling as I beheld the great sight before me: and at that moment when the world came into view, it began to lightning and thunder.

As the lightning flashed over the face of the earth, my eyes went downward and I was facing the north. Suddenly I beheld what looked like a great giant, and as I stared and looked at it, I was almost bewildered by the sight. It was so gigantic and so great. His feet seemed to reach to the north pole and his head to the south. Its arms were stretched from sea to sea. I could not even begin to understand whether this be a mountain or this be a giant, but as I watched, I suddenly beheld a great giant. I could see his head was struggling for life. He wanted to live, but his body was covered with debris from head to foot, and at times this great giant would move his body and act as though it would even raise up at times. And when it did, thousands of little creatures seemed to run away. Hideous creatures would run away from this giant, and when he would become calm, they would come back.

All of a sudden this great giant lifted his hand towards heaven, and then it lifted its other hand, and when it did these creatures by the thousands seemed to flee away from this giant and go into the darkness of the night.

Slowly this great giant began to rise and as he did, his head and hands went into the clouds. As he rose to his feet he seemed to have cleansed himself from the debris and filth that was upon him, and he began to raise his hands into the heavens as though praising the Lord, and as he raised his hands, they went even unto the clouds.

Suddenly, every cloud became silver, the most beautiful silver I have ever known. As I watched this phenomenon it was so great I could not even begin to understand what it all meant. I was so stirred as I watched it, and I cried unto the Lord and I said, "Oh Lord, what is the meaning of this." And I felt as if I was actually in the Spirit and I could feel the presence of the Lord even as I was asleep.

And from those clouds suddenly there came great drops of liquid light raining down upon this mighty giant, and slowly, slowly, this giant began to melt, began to sink itself in the very earth itself, and as he melted, his whole form seemed to have melted upon the face of the earth, and this great rain began to come down. Liquid drops of light began to flood the very earth itself and as I watched this giant that seemed to melt, suddenly it became millions of people over the face of the earth. As I beheld the sight before me, people stood up all over the world! They were lifting their hands and they were praising the Lord.

At that very moment there came a great thunder that seemed to roar from the heavens. I turned my eyes toward the heavens and suddenly I saw a figure in white, in glistening white the most glorious thing that I have ever seen in my entire life. I did not see the face, but somehow I knew it was the Lord Jesus Christ, and he stretched forth his hand, and as he did, he would stretch it forth to one, and to another, and to another. And as he stretched forth his hand upon the nations and the people of the world, men and women, as he pointed toward them, this liquid light seemed to flow from his hands into them, and a mighty anointing of God came upon them, and those people began to go forth in the name of the Lord.

I do not know how long I watched it. It seemed it went into days and weeks and months. And I beheld this Christ as he continued to stretch forth his hand; but there was a tragedy. There were many people as he stretched forth his hand that refused the anointing of God and the call of God. I saw men and women that I knew. People that I felt would certainly receive the call of God. But as he stretched forth his hand toward this one and toward that one, they simply bowed their head and began to back away. And each of those that seemed to bow down and back away, seemed to go into darkness. Blackness seemed to swallow them everywhere.

I was bewildered as I watched it, but these people that he had anointed, hundreds of thousands of people all over the world, in Africa, England, Russia, China, America, all over the world, the anointing of God was upon these people as they went forward in the name of the Lord. I saw these men and women as they went forth. They were ditch diggers, they were washerwomen, they were rich men, they were poor men. I saw people who were bound with paralysis and sickness and blindness and deafness. As the Lord stretched forth to give them this anointing, they became well, they became healed, and they went forth!

And this is the miracle of it, this is the glorious miracle of it, those people would stretch forth their hands exactly as the Lord did, and it seemed as if there was this same liquid fire in their hands. As they stretched forth their hands they said, "According to my word, be thou made whole."

As these people continued in this mighty end-time ministry, I did not fully realize what it was, and I looked to the Lord and said, "What is the meaning of this?" And he said, "This is that which I will do in the last days. I will restore all that the cankerworm, the palmerworm, the caterpiller—I will restore all that they have destroyed. This, my people, in the end times will go forth. As a mighty army shall they sweep over the face of the earth."

As I was at this great height, I could behold the whole world. I watched these people as they were going to and fro over the face of the earth. Suddenly there was a man in Africa and in a moment he was transported by the Spirit of God, and perhaps he was in Russia, or China or America or some other place, and vice versa. All over the world these people went, and they came through fire, and through pestilence, and through famine. Neither fire nor persecution, nothing seemed to stop them.

Angry mobs came to them with swords and with guns. And like Jesus, they passed through the multitudes and they could not find them, but they went forth in the name of the Lord, and everywhere they stretched forth their hands, the sick were healed, the blind eyes were opened. There was not a long prayer, and after I had reviewed the vision many times in my mind, and I thought about it many times, I realised that I never saw a church, and I never saw or heard a denomination, but these people were going in the name of the Lord of Hosts. Hallelujah!

As they marched forth in everything they did as the ministry of Christ in the end times, these people were ministering to the multitudes over the face of the earth. Tens of thousands, even millions seemed to come to the Lord Jesus Christ as these people stood forth and gave the message of the kingdom, of the coming kingdom, in this last hour. It was so glorious, but it seems as though there were those that rebelled, and they would become angry and they tried to attack those workers that were giving the message.

God is going to give the world a demonstration in this last hour as the world has never known. These men and women are of all walks of life, degrees will mean nothing. I saw these workers as they were going over the face of the earth. When one would stumble and fall, another would come and pick him up. There were no "big I" and "little you," but every mountain was brought low and every valley was exalted, and they seemed to have one thing in common—there was a divine love, a divine love that seemed to flow forth from these people as they worked together, and as they lived together. It was the most glorious sight that I have ever known. Jesus Christ was the theme of their life. They continued and it seemed the days went by as I stood and beheld this sight. I could only cry, and sometimes I laughed. It was so wonderful as these people went throughout the face of the whole earth, bringing forth in this last end time.

As I watched from the very heaven itself, there were times when great deluges of this liquid light seemed to fall upon great congregations, and that congregation would lift up their hands and seemingly praise God for hours and even days as the Spirit of God came upon them. God said, "I will pour my Spirit upon all flesh," and that is exactly this thing. And to every man and every woman that received this power, and the anointing of God, the miracles of God, there was no ending to it.

We have talked about miracles. We have talked about signs and wonders, but I could not help but weep as I read again this morning, at 4 o'clock this morning, the letter from our native workers. This is only the evidence of the beginning for one man, a "do-nothing, an unheard-of," who would go and stretch forth his hand and say, "In the name of the Lord Jesus Christ, I command life to flow into your body." I dropped to my knees and began to pray again, and I said, "Lord, I know that this time is coming soon!"

And then again, as these people were going about the face of the earth, a great persecution seemed to come from every angle.

Suddenly there was another great clap of thunder, that seemed to resound around the world, and I heard again the voice, the voice that seemed to speak, "Now this is my people. This is my beloved bride." And when the voice spoke, I looked upon the earth and I could see the lakes and the mountains. The graves were opened and people from all over the world, the saints of all ages, seemed to be rising. And as they rose from the grave, suddenly all these people came from every direction. From the east and the west, from the north and the south, and they seemed to be forming again this gigantic body. As the dead in Christ seemed to be rising first, I could hardly comprehend it. It was so marvellous. It was so far beyond anything I could ever dream or think of.

But as this body suddenly began to form, and take shape again, it took shape again in the form of this mighty giant, but this time it was different. It was arrayed in the most beautiful gorgeous white. Its garments were without spot or wrinkle as its body began to form, and the people of all ages seemed to be gathered into this body, and slowly, slowly, as it began to form up into the very heavens, suddenly from the heavens above, the Lord Jesus came, and became the head, and I heard another clap of thunder that said, "This is my beloved bride for whom I have waited. She will come forth even tried by fire. This is she that I have loved from the beginning of time."

As I watched, my eyes suddenly turned to the far north, and I saw seemingly destruction: men and women in anguish and crying out, and buildings in destruction. Then I heard again, the fourth voice that said, "Now is my wrath being poured out upon the face of the earth." From the ends of the whole world, the wrath of God seemed to be poured out and it seemed that there were great vials of God's wrath being poured out upon the face of the earth. I can remember it as though it happened a moment ago. I shook and trembled as I beheld the awful sight of seeing the cities, and whole nations going down into destruction.

I could hear the weeping and wailing. I could hear people crying. They seemed to cry as they went into caves, but the caves in the mountains opened up.

They leaped into water, but the water would not drown them. There was nothing that could destroy them. They were wanting to take their lives, but they could not. Then again I turned my eyes to this glorious sight, this body arrayed in beautiful white, shining garments. Slowly, slowly, it began to lift from the earth, and as it did, I awoke. What a sight I had beheld! I had seen the end-time ministries of the last hour. Again on July 27, at 2:30 in the morning, the same revelation, the same vision came again exactly as it did before.

My life has been changed as I realised that we are living in that end time, for all over the world God is anointing men and women with this ministry. It will not be doctrine. It will not be a churchianity. It is going to be Jesus Christ. They will give forth the word of the Lord, and are going to say, "I heard it so many times in the vision and according to my word it shall be done."

Endnote

1. Reprinted from *To Heal the Sick*, by Charles and Frances Hunter (Kingwood, Texas: Hunter Books, n.d.), 8-16.

Books to help you grow strong in Jesus

THE GOD CHASERS (Best-selling **Destiny Image** book)
by Tommy Tenney.

There are those so hungry, so desperate for His presence, that they become consumed with finding Him. Their longing for Him moves them to do what they would otherwise never do: Chase God. But what does it really mean to chase God? Can He be "caught"? Is there an end to the thirsting of man's soul for Him? Meet Tommy Tenney—God chaser. Join him in his search for God. Follow him as he ignores the maze of religious tradition and finds himself, not chasing God, but to his utter amazement, caught by the One he had chased.
ISBN 0-7684-2016-4

GOD CHASERS DAILY MEDITATION & PERSONAL JOURNAL
by Tommy Tenney.

Does your heart yearn to have an intimate relationship with your Lord? Perhaps you long to draw closer to your heavenly Father, but you don't know how or where to start. This *Daily Meditation & Personal Journal* will help you begin a journey that will change your life. As you read and journal, you'll find your spirit running to meet Him with a desire and fervor you've never before experienced. Let your heart hunger propel you into the chase of your life…after God!
ISBN 0-7684-2040-7

POWER, HOLINESS, AND EVANGELISM
Contributing Authors: *Gordon Fee, Steve Beard, Dr. Michael Brown, Pablo Bottari, Pablo Deiros, Chris Heuertz, Scott McDermott, Carlos Mraida, Mark Nysewander, Stephen Seamands, Harvey Brown Jr.*
Compiled by *Randy Clark*

Many churches today stress holiness but lack power, while others display great power but are deficient in personal holiness and Christian character. If we really want to win our world for Christ, we must bring both holiness and power back into our lives. A church on fire will draw countless thousands to her light.
ISBN 1-56043-345-0

THE RADICAL CHURCH
by Bryn Jones.

The world of the apostles and the world of today may look a lot different, but there is one thing that has not changed: the need for a radical Church in a degenerate society. We still need a church, a body of people, who will bring a hard-hitting, totally unfamiliar message: Jesus has come to set us free! Bryn Jones of Ansty, Coventry, United Kingdom, an apostolic leader to numerous churches across the world, will challenge your view of what church is and what it is not. Be prepared to learn afresh of the Church that Jesus Christ is building today!
ISBN 0-7684-2022-9

Available at your local Christian bookstore.

For more information and sample chapters, visit www.reapernet.com

5B-2:57

Books to help you grow strong in Jesus